Narrative Thread

Narrative Thread

Conversations on Fashion Collections

Mark C. O'Flaherty

BLOOMSBURY VISUAL ARTS
LONDON • NEW YORK • OXFORD • NEW DELHI • SYDNEY

BLOOMSBURY VISUAL ARTS
Bloomsbury Publishing Plc
50 Bedford Square, London, WC1B 3DP, UK
1385 Broadway, New York, NY 10018, USA
29 Earlsfort Terrace, Dublin 2, Ireland

BLOOMSBURY, BLOOMSBURY VISUAL ARTS and the Diana logo are
trademarks of Bloomsbury Publishing Plc

First published in Great Britain 2023

For legal purposes the Acknowledgments on p. 296 constitute an
extension of this copyright page.

Cover design: Adriana Brioso
Cover image: Sandy Powell, London, 2022, by Mark C. O'Flaherty
Image on p. ii: Desmond is Amazing, Bushwick, New York
Image on p. vi: Waistcoat by John Galliano, *Les Incroyables* collection, graduation show, June 1984.

Bloomsbury Publishing Plc does not have any control over, or responsibility for, any
third-party websites referred to or in this book. All internet addresses given in this
book were correct at the time of going to press. The author and publisher regret
any inconvenience caused if addresses have changed or sites have ceased
to exist, but can accept no responsibility for any such changes.

A catalogue record for this book is available from the British Library.

A catalog record for this book is available from the Library of Congress.

ISBN: HB: 978-1-3502-8767-9
          PB: 978-1-3502-8766-2
          ePDF: 978-1-3502-8768-6
          eBook: 978-1-3502-8769-3

Typeset by Typo•glyphix, Burton-on-Trent, DE14 3HE, UK
Printed and bound in India

To find out more about our authors and books visit www.bloomsbury.com
and sign up for our newsletters.

CONTENTS

Foreword

Reading *Narrative Thread* felt like coming home—home to the scraps and pieces of my life that I have collected to form an ever-changing collage of experience, memory, loss, and love. My wardrobe is an archive that evokes a geography of love. It runs from my earliest memories as a child to the present day. Reading this astounding work inspired me to rethink the story my clothes tell. I was reminded of Miyako Ishiuchi's poignant photographs of her dead mother's clothes, lipstick, hairbrush—shown at the Venice Biennale in 2005—which show us that what we have been in the past may be "traces of the future."

I can remember when I was at Oxford, scouring charity shops for pieces of vintage—a 1920s kimono, a 1930s silk dressing gown—and during the 1980s I was often at Laurence Corner finding sailor jackets and parachute silk. I don't think we change. Decades later I am still drawn to Diane Ashman's incredible shop in Welshpool to source 1920s slipper satin wedding dresses, which I wear in layers with a kimono.

Our clothes inevitably tell our story, describing us in a way we are hardly aware of until we stand back and look. Everybody makes a creative act when they get dressed, from the choice of trainers to the escape of wearing black. Whether we dress to protect ourselves or to project ourselves, dressing is transformative.

Sometimes I think we hold on to clothes because we do not want the emotion still reverberating within them to fade. I play them like piano notes, each dress a different tone, each shoe a different key. Together they are the melody of my life. They are versions of ourselves that hang in wardrobes and attics like a Boro Furoshiki wrap cloth: so many swatches of feeling. What remains is what is left of us—the hopes and the fears and the joyous vertices of abandon traced in a frayed hem. I can still catch a faint scent of Fracas when I run my hand over a Galliano gray chiffon ghost dress. I can still remember dancing at a Met after-party in a Chanel couture shadow dress, its delicate diamonds of graphite mousseline peeling off the narrow skirt as testament to the wildness of the night.

This book will fascinate and excite but also make you reconsider and refine what you might have taken for granted. We are all haunted by who we have been—we wouldn't be who we are otherwise. Our clothes bear witness to our rite of passage, our voyage through cloth.

Amanda Harlech

White lace cage skirt by Comme des Garçons,
White Drama collection, Spring/Summer 2012.

What Do Our Clothes Really Mean?

When Louise Bourgeois lost her husband in 1973, she turned grief and the embroidered handkerchiefs that had been boxed up in her wedding trousseau into art. She hacked into the fabric and began to make a series of cathartic *Woven Drawings* that traced a line back to a childhood spent in her parents' tapestry restoration workshop in a suburb of Paris. Three decades later, she took her favorite clothing and cut it up to create *Ode à la Bièvre* (2002), a series of stitched portraits, assembled as a book. In both instances, the sacrifice was significant. In an interview with Paulo Herkenhoff for a monograph of her work in 2003, she suggested that "you can retell your life and remember your life by the shape, the weight, the color, the smell of the clothes in your closet. Fashion is like the weather, the ocean—it changes all the time."[1] Clothes give shape and form to our lives—from the cloak that Aleister Crowley believed gave him the power of invisibility as he moved at a glacial pace, entirely visible, through the Café Royal in the 1930s, to the 100 identical black turtleneck sweaters that Steve Jobs ordered from Issey Miyake to give him an inexhaustible core component for his perfect uniform. For some artists who use clothing in their work, the power of those objects depends on the wearer being present. Bourgeois's artworks live on and have gained resonance because she took control of their raw materials and reworked them into something else, the destruction of the clothing bringing to mind Robert Rauschenberg's *Erased de Kooning Drawing* (1953). Post-punk author Kathy Acker used clothing the same way she used the literary cut-up technique pioneered by William Burroughs and Brion Gysin, layering herself in contrasting pieces by different designers. Her greatest work was herself:

Wool and taffeta blazer by Jean Paul Gaultier Hommes,
Chic Rabbis collection, Autumn/Winter 1993.

she wanted to be the most modern, provocative person alive. After Acker's death in 1997, the photographer Kaucyila Brooke shot 154 pieces from her wardrobe, including jackets and dresses by Jean Paul Gaultier and Vivienne Westwood, each on a wire hanger and white background. Brooke crudely animated the pieces for each shot using thread, pulling the fabric in different directions. In Acker's absence, however, the clothing too felt lost. The imagery is compelling as documentary, but without their wearer the clothes appear abandoned as much as elegiac.

We hold on to things for obvious reasons—a child's first pair of shoes, or the alpaca overcoat inherited from a parent and imprinted with the faint smell of a long-discontinued fragrance. At other times clothes take root in our lives via less direct paths, and it's not apparent why. They acquire a meaning greater than their function, or flattery of form. Sometimes, without it being intended, a wardrobe becomes a collection, and the patina it develops—even if barely perceptible—tells stories.

This book is a collection of conversations and shoots with individuals whose relationship with clothes has created something significant in their lives. It is about how they have used these objects to develop narratives. It is also about our relationship with fashion over the decades, and the changing nature of it as commodity. Fundamentally fashion is product, but it brings us identity and memory.

What gives a garment longevity? Sometimes it is a sense of authenticity and romanticism, afforded by construction that costs more than might be seen as essential, or by reworking ideas from history. Sometimes it's the feel of a certain fabric, a nuanced twist on tailoring or something extreme that reads as transgressive. It could just be about where you found a garment or who gave it to you. Fashion is about feeling that something can represent you and tell your story.

I've spent twenty-five years photographing and interviewing people with the goal of revealing and documenting what makes them who they are. While I have a personal connection with the subjects in this book, none of them had been asked before about the most private aspects of the clothes they own or examined their meaning in this much detail. In talking to and photographing the individuals featured in this book, I wanted to explore through words and pictures what makes the pieces they own special, and where the power inherent in each one comes from. (Sometimes a garment was too sensitive: one man didn't want a certain jacket he owned to be photographed because he planned to wear it for his wedding. Even though the event would come before publication, it didn't feel right to him: if I photographed the jacket before his wedding day, it wouldn't be the same jacket as after.)

The resonance attached to a garment has been key to the way fashion has been marketed since the days of the House of Worth in the nineteenth century. By stitching his name—as opposed to that of his client—into a garment, Charles Frederick Worth established a new power structure in fashion. That audacity would define the future of the industry. It is impossible now to talk about our relationship to clothes without considering our relationship with the idea of the designer, and how that creates meaning even before you consider buying something. Of course, everything has always been "designed"; no artifact goes straight into production. But in 1947 you weren't just buying the "New Look," you were buying the physical manifestation of Christian Dior's genius. You were investing in, and wearing, an idea. The implication was that the idea was Dior's, and Dior's alone.

In the twentieth century, the designer increasingly became more important than the client. As we moved into the twenty-first century, the elitism of the designer as deity—and the veneration of products attached to them as sacred relics—was diluted to target the broadest markets possible. The concept of the designer became abstract, as zombie brands bearing the name of long-retired or dead men recruited new talent to create fresh product and content for media that bore little or no relation to the original idea on which the business was founded. Chain store collaborations, and the demise of bricks and mortar as retail shifted online, led to a critical mass of branding. Apart from the overnight queue of people intent on securing one of those branded items, and the various Dover Street Markets around the world as well as genuine thrift and vintage markets, fashion is no longer consumed as part of a physical and social experience, as it was at Biba, Fiorucci, and Sign of the Times in decades past. Now, things must stand out on a screen to shift units, as exemplified by the new and aggressively lurid "non colors" developed by sportswear brands, which consist of a weave or blend designed to arrest your attention as you scroll. Their sole purpose is to stop traffic. The graphic power of a physical product is one thing, but now we have virtual product as part of the metaverse. You shop for your avatar. It still means buying into an idea but dispenses with the physical product. It is preposterous but has a strange logic: you indulge a fantasy, it has an accessible price point, and, apart from the CO_2 emissions attributable to digital activity, it's sustainable.

Technology, along with the terminal decline of traditional office culture and the uniform it required, has generated some remarkable new design. But the reality of fashion as an industry means that it is driven by product that is rigorously tested via focus groups and trend forecasting. Long-term emotional connection is less a consideration than initial impact. It's easy to look down at fashion as frivolous and ephemeral—which it can be—and as an increasingly cynical business, which it certainly is. There's no other industry that has made itself not just resilient to criticism but managed to virtually eradicate it through manipulation of the media it is married to. The emperor must always have new clothes because new things make money, and criticism is permissible only in an opaque way. Damnation comes solely in the form of faint praise. And yet, alongside, we have been forced to consider the environmental and social impacts of buying garments with a limited lifespan and often produced in scandalous, inhumane conditions. There has been a divergence between fast fashion and niche artisanal craft, with an ever-growing appreciation of vintage clothing. Clothes have become important in ways that hadn't been considered before. It is now a moral as well as emotional obligation not to throw something away.

The individuals in the following pages see the clothing they own as profoundly significant. They have a dynamic relationship with it, and that relationship is constantly changing because fashion and society are changing. One of the inspirations for this book came from research I was doing at the Westminster Menswear Archive at the University of Westminster, which was established in 2016 by Professor Andrew Groves. Here are racks of garments that tell thousands of stories, from military (I discovered that British soldiers call U.S. kit "Gucci" because it is so well made) to fashion/tech hybrid pieces, like turn-of-the-century C.P. Company jackets that incorporated cutting-edge technology, including Sony Discmans. Those pieces, created at a time when everyone was excited to be moving into a new century, represent social history. Of course, the future didn't look like C.P. Company predicted, and every piece of tech incorporated in those jackets would go on to become an anachronism—but doesn't that make them more interesting? It's the old adage of nothing being as boring as yesterday's newspaper, but nothing as interesting as one from 100 years ago.

Further inspiration came from a day spent with Carla Sozzani, the founder of 10 Corso Como. I was with her in Paris as she prepared a posthumous retrospective of the work of her close friend and collaborator Azzedine Alaïa. Sozzani talked about an extensive collection of the couture he had made for her—an emotional topic, particularly as Azzedine had then only recently died. She also talked about how important Alaïa's own collection of couture by other designers had been to him. As some people collect paintings, so others collect gowns, many of which have been crafted by methods more meticulous and detailed than any pointillism.

I began to think about collections of fashion in private hands as opposed to institutions, and what those garments meant to their owners. How had these items defined certain eras, occasions, and people for them? How had they subsequently inspired their own work?

As I went through what I owned personally, I thought about what each piece meant to me. If it was ten, twenty, or even thirty years old, why had it survived numerous culls? I opened a box containing a cerise cycling top with Cyrillic script from Jean Paul Gaultier's 1986 *Russian Constructivist* collection, various pieces by Issey Miyake that I had bought in the sales at Jones on Floral Street, and a hand-painted T-shirt by Stephen Sprouse I'd bought at the Diesel store in Union Square in 2003, a few months before the designer died. At one end of my wardrobe, sealed up in suit carriers studded with cedar discs to ward off moths, hung priestly tailoring from John Rocha's much missed shop on London's Dover Street, several jackets by Todd Lynn from limited editions of five or ten, and an Alexander McQueen jacket from his 1996 *Dante* collection, now two sizes too small for my frame. There were also various pieces by Richmond Cornejo, Comme des Garçons, and Helmut Lang, and badges from

Keith Haring's Pop Shop, Tokyo Boogie Beat, and World. A lot of these items are captured in photographs I have of me, stored in various boxes along with club flyers and party and show invitations. These things were an integral part of nights in the 1980s and 1990s at Ascension and Kinky Gerlinky in London, and Jackie 60 and The Sound Factory in New York. They remind me of a time when I would wear color and pattern, long abandoned through fear and practicality (I've never grasped what colors suit me—and besides, it's easier when you travel constantly to just stick to black). Some of what I get from those old clothes is a feeling of nostalgia—clothes from our past are interesting because they represent who we were and, looking at a lot of my collection, I could see the difference between youth and middle age. But it's not just that. Buying clothes in the 1980s and 1990s, whether vintage or new, wasn't just about shopping: it was ritual. You had to experience them in person.

Before the broader commodification of what was once considered elite, desire for clothing was fostered in a nuanced way. Clothes were mythologized in magazines, but the actual product was often scarce, produced in small quantities by designers in their own studios, and difficult to come by. You might have wanted to buy a pair of John Moore shoes or a Chris Nemeth jacket at the House of Beauty and Culture in Dalston, but it seemed to be perpetually closed. Abstract notions of design and aesthetics took on more importance than actualization. Like many people I knew at the time, I didn't just buy something: I would fixate on it and strategize, revisiting a Comme des Garçons or John Galliano jacket weekly until, if funds and the sale gods allowed, I was able to purchase it. I remember going to the first Yohji Yamamoto store in London in the 1980s, on South Molton Street. If it was intimidating to walk into that small, awkward space, where rows of white shirts and voluminous black coats hung at exaggerated distances from one another, then to touch the garments felt, for someone obsessed with the story behind them, like contact with artifacts from another universe. They were afforded the reverence of Joseph Beuys felt suits in a museum. Yohji wanted to democratize fashion and create new kinds of uniforms, hence the institutional white shirts and black tailoring, but the price for that kind of democracy, once it had been flown from Japan and cleared UK customs, was ruinous. With little in the way of actual clothing detail to focus on, apart from a sense that each item was flawlessly executed, I remember being transfixed by the gray rectangular labels sewn into those austere garments—Yamamoto's signature finely woven on to each panel, with "MADE IN JAPAN," the fabric composition (customarily rayon) and dry-cleaning instructions detailed below in sans serif. The first piece of Yohji I owned was an oversized woven gray shirt that hung like a robe to just above my knee. It looked monastic, and I bought it for £30, second- or third-hand from Camden Market. Putting it on felt powerful because it came from that other universe, which existed largely in my imagination.

There are still designers working in fashion who insist on physical contact with their work before you can buy it, and who have nothing to do with the instant gratification of getting this week's hyped collaboration between a sportswear and luxury brand. Karim Fares of Archivio J.M. Ribot and the reclusive British designer Paul Harnden sell to only a few retailers worldwide, and nothing is available online. Everything John Alexander Skelton produces is numbered and produced in short runs; he refuses to sell through e-commerce, and each collection is highly personal. Skelton sees what he does as political, exploring class and society and how both relate to fashion; he has created collections that investigate pre-industrial revolution folk culture, and the Peterloo Massacre of 1819, an event that created seismic changes in Westminster and in the industrial North, after a cavalry regiment charged, bearing swords, into a crowd of 60,000 protestors. Many of those in attendance were workers from the textile industry who had assembled in Manchester demanding parliamentary reform and the right to vote. Skelton's politics are further reflected in his production, which uses dyeing and unusual weaving techniques long discarded by modern manufacturers.

I am fascinated by the way clothing creates physical connections between people. It's something Louise Bourgeois explored back in 1978 with *A Banquet/A Fashion Show of Body Parts*, a performance piece which involved wrapping people in white fabric that had been cut and padded to incorporate breast shapes—an event that would be an inspiration for Rei Kawakubo's work in the mid-2000s. In 1994, I took part in Adam Chodzko's artwork *Product Recall*, in which a group of owners of Vivienne Westwood's Clint Eastwood bomber jacket, with its elongated knitted sleeves and body, were filmed socializing at a derelict space off the Charing Cross Road. Like everyone else there, I had bought my jacket in the mid-1980s. We had been alerted to the event by flyposters around Soho and adverts in *i-D* magazine, which featured an image of the design on a figure with a blurred-out face, and a contact number. As Chodzko—who was fascinated by the jacket but didn't actually own one himself—has explained, "'Recall' refers to the process of remembering as well as a literal recalling of a product; both are a form of 'drawing into' the present":

> The request … appeared to be, stylistically, somewhere between a religious reunion or cult ritual … The poster announces that 'it has been discovered that this design was based on an early scheme for a memory jacket,' but without clarifying whether this quality is just passing information or the reason for the urgency of the Product Recall. It suggests (as does the 'aura' within the visual imagery) that the jacket might possess powers, a magical item derived from a fairy tale, ancient myth, or science fiction.[2]

Hussein Chalayan incorporated something similar into his Autumn/Winter 2003 menswear collection, *Place/Non-Place*. The internal labels on one of the outerwear designs invited owners to come to Heathrow Airport on May 4, 2004 for an unspecified reason, giving each garment a sense of time, occasion, and purpose. It was an examination of the strangeness of the airport as a place to gather—a "non-place," in Marc Augé's coinage.[3] The invitation was also an extension of the collection itself. Only one person turned up to Heathrow for the Chalayan event in 2004, because the garment was brand new and hadn't developed meaning or earned its place in anyone's life. But the idea was enough for Chalayan. Of course, if Supreme replicated this in the 2020s, the airport would be overwhelmed. The fascination with a designer's imagination and storytelling is nothing compared to the excitement engineered by a hype brand.

Another event based on the shared experience of a single garment—in this case the Sleeping Bag Coat by Norma Kamali—took the form of a flashmob at midday on May 17, 1983 at the junction of Broad Street and Wall Street in Manhattan. Dozens of people who had bought one of the coats in the ten years since it had first gone on sale were filmed running around the area. They were recorded telling stories about the significance of the garment in their lives, from its part in sexual liaisons to one woman's account of using her coat to create a comfortable place for her cat to have kittens. Unlike Chalayan's intellectual statement, the Kamali flashmob was a simple celebration of memories linked to a much-loved garment.

While this book is about how clothing creates a narrative for its owner, it also addresses the stories being told by designers. The surrealist fantasy of Schiaparelli is just one facet of high fashion. To suggest that fashion is aloof from the realities of the world is to overlook those designers whose work has made incisive, sometimes confrontational statements. Alexander McQueen's *Highland Rape* collection of 1995 was an impassioned retelling of the Highland Clearances through the medium of the runway. In 1971, Yves Saint Laurent agitated press and buyers with his purposely bleak *Mourning for Vietnam* collection, and in 1995 the Comme des Garçons Homme Plus *Sleep* collection made front page news around the world for its use of imagery synonymous with the Holocaust, including striped pajamas and bootprints on fabric. Rei Kawakubo denied any awareness of the connection but, inadvertent or not, it was impossible to interpret the imagery as benign.

The twenty-first century brought with it a surge of new polemic. Demna Gvasalia's 2020 show for Balenciaga was themed on climate change: models appeared in latex trench coats while the front three rows of seats were partially submerged underwater, rendering them unusable for guests. The message wasn't subtle: climate changing is coming for you, no matter what your privilege. For most of her career to date, Marine Serre has been using elaborately recycled fabrics and presenting her clothing in a dystopian, menacing context, fueled by the anxiety of climate change. She was swift to react to the pandemic in 2020 with film work that incorporated masks, medical procedures, and invasive surgical implements reminiscent of David Cronenberg at his most clinical. There are parallels to be drawn between the circularity of Serre's work and that of Walid al Damirji, whose By Walid label is sewn into clothing made from antique fabrics. But Walid's clothing is deeply romantic, and his ongoing search for unique fabrics means production is inherently limited: whether it's a jacket cut from an old French mail bag or a coat that's a patchwork of nineteenth-century Chinese embroidered silk, the clothes he makes have been a part of several lives already.

For designers who share in this consciousness, the people involved in the production process are part of their story. Bethany Williams works almost wholly with recycled and deadstock textiles and uses her practice to create community change as well as luxury product to sell to an elite consumer. She has employed women from HMP Downview to sew garments, and when the Covid-19 pandemic shut London down in 2020 and it was clear that frontline NHS staff hadn't been equipped with sufficient PPE, she joined forces with friends from the industry—Phoebe English, Holly Fulton, and Cozette McCreery—to create the Emergency Designer Network, producing and supplying protective wear to doctors and nurses. Focused once more on her own label, Williams has commissioned her mother to create handknits for her collections. There is an intimacy implied in those garments that is rare in commercial fashion. For anyone buying a garment, this kind of provenance is poignant. How something comes into being has profound meaning, whether that's because of who stitched it, or how it was presented on the catwalk.

Sometimes the meaning of an item has little to do with the design and everything to do with circumstance. In August 2020 Philip Stephens, the designer of the London-based label Unconditional, died suddenly. We had been close friends since I was a teenager and we had worked together repeatedly. The night before he died, we had been exchanging text messages and, despite years of personal challenges, it sounded like things were getting better for both him and his family. All of this made the news of his passing more difficult to accept. Philip had gifted me numerous things over the years, and on the day I heard that he had passed away, I unfolded a piece of Unconditional gray cashmere only to discover it had been devoured by moths. It seemed beyond repair. There were more holes than fabric. But I had it restored as best I could and will never part with it. Louise Bourgeois makes the case for the power of clothing in our lives, in the most poetic way I've encountered to date: "I've always had a fascination with the needle, the magic power of the needle. The needle is used to repair damage. It's a claim to forgiveness. It is never aggressive, it's not a pin."[4] I love the ragged mess that's left of my cashmere from Philip and I will continue to repair it as necessary, until I'm also gone.

There are many things I regret letting go of. The numerous pieces of Vivienne Westwood star-print denim from her 1985 *Mini-Crini* collection that I sold because I felt they represented a part of my life that was over. The BodyMap knit I let a friend borrow and never saw again. That Yohji overshirt that would have suited the 50-year-old me more than the 25-year-old who found it in Camden Market. This book is about the stories behind the clothes from our past and how they shape our present and future. It's about what we hold on to and why, and how those garments tell us and others who we are.

Mark C. O'Flaherty

NOTES

1   Herkenhoff, Paulo (2004), "Interview: Paulo Herkenhoff in conversation with Louise Bourgeois" in *Louise Bourgeois*, 22, London and New York: Phaidon Press.

2   See www.adamchodzko.com/works/product-recall-1994 (accessed 30 January 2023).

3   Augé, Marc (1995), *Non-places: Introduction to an Anthropology of Supermodernity*, trans. John Howe, London and New York: Verso.

4   Bernadac, Marie-Louise and Hans-Ulrich Obrist, eds (1998), *Louise Bourgeois: Destruction of the Father/Reconstruction of the Father, Writings and Interviews 1923–1997*, 222, London: Violette Editions.

Valerie Steele
Fashion as Product

Valerie Steele is Director and Chief Curator of the Museum at the Fashion Institute of Technology (FIT) in New York City. She is the author or co-author of numerous books and has curated more than twenty-five exhibitions.

MARK: Has fashion become product more than design?

VALERIE: Fashion has always been "product." It is a commodity. Because capitalism, like the bourgeoisie, has been rising for centuries, there has been fashion product at least since the Renaissance. The specialized production of dress and textiles, along with global trade routes, goes back millennia, so to imagine that clothing fashions were once pure artisanal craft is just a romanticized William Morris version of the past.

MARK: But are we seeing a change in the commodification of fashion?

VALERIE: Well, it's all a matter of degree. I do think that our particular stage in capitalism has seen hyper-commodification, with clothes being mass produced and globally distributed in astronomical numbers. We can't call it "late stage capitalism," because we don't know if it's near the end or not. But we have had branding in fashion since before the House of Worth in the 1850s, and named creators go back even further: think of Rose Bertin, who was known as the Minister of Fashion to Marie Antoinette.

Valerie Steele at FIT, New York.

MARK: Some people would say there's a chasm between aggressively commercialized product and authentic craft.

VALERIE: Authenticity is a chimera. You run after this mythical beast, but it's not really there, it's part of a fantasy. On the other hand, we can feel it when something seems flagrantly inauthentic. It's natural to look back and see fashion as having been less commodified in the past, but that impulse is partly nostalgic. As Talleyrand said: "He who has not lived before the Revolution [i.e. before 1789] does not know the sweetness of life and cannot imagine that there can be happiness in life."

MARK: Can you be a designer today without commodification?

VALERIE: The issue with designers isn't that they brand their work, but that they are increasingly pushed to become part of a vast conglomerate. The independent designer is an endangered species because the fashion world is increasingly divided into luxury conglomerates and fast fashion conglomerates, and it's getting harder for designers to exist in that space between the two. To exist, you have to brand yourself.

MARK: There are designers who rail against that, though—who work on small-scale production and only want to sell to a few stores.

VALERIE: And those are brands. They are branding themselves as anti-brand and anti-fashion, which is something that has been incorporated into fashion for decades. I remember years ago asking a group of leather fetishists what they thought of the most recent Versace show, and they said they hated it. I asked them why, because it was beautiful—essentially a high-quality version of what they were all wearing. "Yes," one replied, "but people used to dress this way because it meant something, not because it was a fashion statement." Unfortunately for the members of subcultures, fashion is like a giant vacuum cleaner that hoovers up all the cool looks.

MARK: What about when something prosaic is stamped with a logo? The collaboration between Prada and Adidas in 2019 comes to mind.

VALERIE: Well, it reminds me of Duchamp: a mass-produced toilet is art because the artist says it is. But the concept of the designer sneaker or collaboration also fits in with the whole high/low phenomenon, which has been with us since the early 1960s in the art world. People were horrified that artists like Warhol were painting soup cans. It seemed so low and debased to the Frankfurt School crowd, who saw it as kitsch.

MARK: Did we a see a seismic shift in fashion as product when Yves Saint Laurent introduced ready to wear in 1966?

VALERIE: He was an early adopter, but he wasn't the only one. Pierre Cardin was another couturier who had been experimenting with ready to wear. I don't think that it was the beginning of an end, because in a lot of ways, modern French ready to wear renewed fashion. A lot of the haute couture at the time was old-fashioned—it wasn't all Balenciaga. There were plenty of couturiers who were just churning out product. Yes, it was being sewn by hand, but it wasn't special.

MARK: Can you expand a fashion brand via commercial product but still retain its core values?

VALERIE: Notoriously, Cardin's licensing was insane—904 licenses at its peak, from telephones to toilet paper. When you expand licensing like that, it becomes flagrantly inauthentic, because it's not from the designer's mind or hand. But a lot of creation is a team effort. Many years ago Richard Martin, who was director of the Museum at FIT before he became head of the Costume Institute at the Metropolitan Museum of Art, talked about how it had become common to fetishize the designer as the great artist. The reality is that artists from Raphael onwards were working with a team in a studio. Another reality is that certain things, like accessories, are the moneymakers for a brand. So, you have a situation where the most interesting things, like certain experimental runway looks, aren't even commercially produced. And if something isn't produced, is that really the designer's core idea? I think something has to get off the runway to actually exist as fashion, even if the only person who wears an extreme runway look is a fearless fashion person like Daphne Guinness.

MARK: And when the world of high fashion collaborates with fast fashion to create product—what does that give us?

VALERIE: It severs certain links to core values. LemLem was established by the Ethiopian model Liya Kebede to create clothes made by artisans in Africa. When LemLem partnered with H&M in 2021, the product obviously wasn't being made by those artisans. But the collaboration does drive people to recognize the name, so I believe Kebede, like most independent designers in this position, saw the collaboration as an advertisement for LemLem, which would entice people to buy the real product later. Realistically, though, for a lot of consumers, the H&M garment is all they'll get.

Andre Walker
Fashion and Identity

Brooklyn-based Andre Walker has been designing for over three decades. He has acted as a consultant for Marc Jacobs and Kim Jones and has his own womenswear label, And Re Walker, distributed via Dover Street Market in conjunction with Comme des Garçons.

MARK: How do you think fashion defines identity?

ANDRE: At fifteen I was being heavily influenced by Europe, but I had already been interested in fashion since I was seven years old. A lot of that was down to obsessively reading *W* magazine and looking at the designs of Pablo and Delia, Vivienne Westwood, Zandra Rhodes, Thierry Mugler, Anne Marie Beretta, Walter Albini, Giorgio Armani, and Gianfranco Ferré. And I was buying these clothes then! In 1979 I was already selling T-shirts outside my mother's store and money wasn't an issue. I was fifteen, I had $200 in my pocket and I didn't pay rent, so I went shopping at IF Soho and Charivari.

MARK: You appear in one of Amy Arbus's photographs that was published in 1983 as part of her regular *Village Voice* "On the Street" column. Her work documented various aspects of streetstyle in the post-punk world. A young Madonna was captured the same year as part of the same series. In your portrait you are wearing shorts with a matching elongated waistcoat and sandals over socks with garters. Did you already know who you were going to be at this point, and had you already constructed an image of who that was?

Andre Walker in his home studio in Prospect Park, Brooklyn, New York.

ANDRE: I definitely already knew I wanted to be a designer. First I imitated *W*, then I started buying *Vogue Italia* and *Vogue Paris*. Clothing was an extension of my life from the magazines—in my head I'd already assumed I was an international star designer. I was furious that I couldn't go to Studio 54, and I missed the disco boat, so by the time I was fifteen I was ready to hit the town. My first clubs were Club Berlin, then the Roxy and Danceteria. But yes, I was creating a persona for the night. I'd call it "self-dictatorship visual authoritarian."

At fifteen you don't know the culture, but you know the tropes. All my high school friends were smarty-pants, we were all nerds. There was a store I used to go to called Sohozat down on West Broadway, which sold labels from London like PX and Axiom, and I'd buy copies of *i-D* there. I became familiar with the concept of streetstyle, whether it was New Romantic or ska, or bands like the Fun Boy Three and Haircut 100. I was always aware of the incremental changes in the British style scene.

MARK: These are all quite tribal things you're talking about. Were you personally mixing it up or quite focused on one thing?

ANDRE: The *i-D* generation, the Fiorucci and Studio 54 generations, they were subcultural, but they attracted iconoclasts and misfits. So actually, a lot of us were crafting our own distinct and individual looks. Look at *i-D* in the 1980s, and you see the social templates that created the music, fashion, and territory.

MARK: Has that all remained in the last century?

ANDRE: No, it's here more today, because of social media. The only thing missing is the music. There's no real scene to go with music, and music is no longer look-specific. Back then, musicians from the ska or rockabilly scene influenced what you wore, but I feel that luxury, identity, subculture, and music have kind of melded now into a semi-indiscernible state where you have many ideals converging at once. The more recognizable subcultures like goth and punk have fused with technology, televised fantasy, and other elements to further blur their origins.

MARK: It's interesting how clothing linked inherently to music is so distinct and strong, like Stephen Sprouse with Debbie Harry, and when Malcolm McLaren worked with Vivienne Westwood.

ANDRE: Absolutely. Malcolm and Vivienne were married to music circa punk and Seditionaries, and then the Nostalgia of Mud store and "Buffalo Gals," and then Malcolm went off to the vogue and ball scene, and things got divorced. The fashion changed and lost some of its intent.

MARK: There are still designers who have strong links with music. Virgil Abloh was a DJ, and music felt linked to what he was doing with Off-White, and then Vuitton, and a certain hip-hop lifestyle.

ANDRE: Virgil had a grasp of his audience, and the look was about aspirational consumption, or expression. But I'm not sure if that's just because of the social status it afforded his audience.

MARK: Are we still using style as a way to rebel as much as to create an identity?

ANDRE: Of course. Let's say I go out with a green clay face mask to go shopping. It looks challenging, but so what? It means I don't have to worry about time—I can go to the supermarket, keep my mask on, come back, and my day hasn't been interrupted. That's a kind of rebellion involving a choice of place and function.

Right now, posing and the apparent imposter syndrome thing is popular. People love inhabiting different personalities, they love elaborating on different aspects of themselves and their image. In fashion we are taught and trained how to do this. We have realized you can't sell trends as easily anymore—now a trend can last for a few minutes before trickling down to places that are remote, but there won't be a huge difference between the support and consumption of the trend because of the technology around it. If you can access it, you can do as you wish. Look at Instagram or *Black Mirror*. We are living in the cult of the individual. And that is being crept up on by biotech and automation. The concept of the self, and community awareness, affect our interpretation of things.

MARK: How will fashion respond to the cult of individuality and the continual expansion of diversity?

ANDRE: It has already happened. You have Carlos Nazario [the Afro-Latino stylist who dressed Lizzo in a red Valentino dress for *Vogue* in 2020] and Ibrahim Kamara [the editor-in-chief of *Dazed* who fled Sierra Leone during the civil war], and many other people working in this area. The question is no longer about individuality, that's a no-brainer. Condé Nast is now amalgamated, and other power centers have supplanted it as a means of expression. Thank God for Dover Street Market—they reminded me that I am a designer.

We are seeing more fashion created from this perspective. Back in 2000 I showed a collection in Paris called *RASTA—Recreational Agreements Surrounding Taste Appreciations*, which incorporated a lot of different Afro-Caribbean design inspiration and influences. I was using them for their aesthetic qualities but also because I feel connected to them. At the same time, I also feel connected to Hollywood, and I also feel connected to historicism. Why should I not love white skin? Why should I not love jet-black skin and otherwise? Why can't I love an Indian person? Why does it have to be a cultural statement? Why can't it be a humanitarian or existential statement?

MARK: What will happen with the binary distinctions that have steered fashion for centuries?

ANDRE: Clothes are inanimate objects. A garment can be worn or designed by anyone. Trying to understand a group of people within society through their use of clothing is interesting on an intellectual level, but apart from creating generalizations about that culture, what does it actually do? I mean—skirts for all, dresses for all, suits for all, bikinis for all. Change is inevitable.

MARK: Media has changed the pace of things. When print media reported on the bourgeoisie Paninaro youth cults in the 1980s in Italy, wearing their pastel, Stone Island, and Moncler and hanging around McDonald's in Rome, and when those magazines did ten-page spreads on whatever was going on in Tokyo, it took months to get to us. Now it's on social media instantly. Is this changing the international nature of fashion and how trends spread?

ANDRE: Well, the whole cultural appropriation issue is one that annoys me when it's discussed. I believe there is a secret desire among a lot of the people in the world to keep things segregated. The uproar about the braids on men on a Comme des Garçons Homme Plus show was idiotic and perverse. I don't have a problem with any of that. I am counterculture in my views—I grew up with Black punks, white punks, and Chinese punks, white and Black New Romantics. I don't think about race. It's not that I am colorblind, it's just that I am just more interested in the epistemology of things. When I was growing up, I didn't know I was "Black." I had no idea and I enjoyed that freedom. I think that it's a privilege to be mindless of your color. I worked with designer Willi Smith, who just happened to be Black, and I really loved what he was doing because he was behaving in a European way, in the same way as Saint Laurent, Kenzo, Givenchy, Thierry Mugler, and Claude Montana. The Parisian designers behaved as if there was no such thing as race. They were addressing the diversity of the population, its traditions, and subcultures.

In a sense it is hilarious how we all accumulate these takes on culture and then frame them from such personal points of view. It's influenced by something more than visual and cultural awareness. Notoriety and exposure have melded with data accumulation to both widen and narrow the eye in a more homogenous embrace of once segregated visual ideals. So yes, it has changed the how and why of the spread of trends.

Claire Wilcox
Fashion and Memory

Claire Wilcox is Chair in Fashion Curation at London College of Fashion, UK. She was Senior Curator of Fashion at the V&A in London from 2004 until 2022, where she curated a series of major shows including *Alexander McQueen: Savage Beauty* (2015), *Frida Kahlo: Making Herself Up* (2018), *Fashioning Masculinities* (2022), and a retrospective of the work of Vivienne Westwood (2004). In 2020 she published a memoir, *Patch Work: A Life Amongst Clothes*.

MARK: Why do we keep clothes, beyond their function and purpose?

CLAIRE: It seems to me inevitable that memory can become embedded in the fibers of the garments we wear. Like Proust with his madeleine, the recollection or feel of a certain garment can trigger involuntary thoughts of the past. But what I find particularly interesting is that there's both an internal and external reality at play, an entanglement of lived experience with how we fashion ourselves. We have an idea of how we look and who we are in our clothes, but even if we look in a mirror, we aren't seeing what other people see. So, clothing becomes a metaphor for who we want to be. It's communicating an important message. We keep things for who we thought we were.

MARK: Clothing with a personal history can, of course, be emotionally charged.

CLAIRE: Speaking personally, I can look at my past life through the lens of different clothes. My mother was a dressmaker and made a lot of pieces for me. I found the attention irksome at the time because I had to stand

Claire Wilcox in the National Art Library, the V&A, London.

still while she was fitting things on my body, but on reflection it was an expression of affection from someone who was normally very reserved. And everything felt special. I remember a blue velvet dress with a white swansdown collar that she made for my birthday party. I was swinging in a hammock in the garden with my friends, and we all fell out into the mud. I felt such grief.

MARK: In terms of clothing and the memory attached to them, can there be anything but melancholy? We always look back on our lives with rose-tinted glasses; the past is past. And when it comes to the clothes of loved ones, it's more poignant. I couldn't look at any of my mother's clothes after she died. I wanted them to disappear.

CLAIRE: When it comes down to emotion, and love and loss, clothing takes on greater weight. Of course, garments aren't manufactured with it. They gain resonance through wear. I always associated my father with a particular texture of clothing—we remember things through all the senses, including touch. In *Patch Work* I wrote about the feel of his woolen jumpers, and it's impossible for me to let go of the last of those. It is a reassurance to me. He was once here, and he still is, on some level. Some clothes have a more obvious emotional lifespan—a wedding dress, for example, is imbued with symbolism. It's like a mayfly. It lives for a day. But it's sometimes the humblest of garments that carry the most emotional weight.

MARK: There is a wonderful story in your book about a pair of early nineteenth-century breeches in the V&A archive, which were part of a wedding outfit belonging to a man who drowned at sea. The entry made by the curator who catalogued them describes a detail in their fabric: "tight gathers, which resemble ripples on a sandy beach after the tide has retreated." In the chapter, you explain how you examined the garment and found that the stitching does indeed look like that, and how moved you were by the metaphor. I wonder, immersing yourself in the past so much, do you feel surrounded by ghosts of sorts?

CLAIRE: I don't feel it as a kind of haunting because these aren't my memories. When I'm working with these pieces, I am objective. I don't feel melancholy, I feel at peace. The past informs the present in a positive way. The past is calm. And once an object is in the museum, it becomes part of the continuum of history. In some ways, the burden of memory can be let go. The museum takes on that responsibility.

MARK: Why is it important that we archive clothing in an institution?

CLAIRE: It's a way to understand the past, present, and future through artifacts that are intimately associated with identity. Going back to Proust, if you read *In Search of Lost Time* when you are sixteen, it will resonate in a totally different way from how it does decades later. Today, I appreciate the accrual of memory. It's an internal resource for a writer—a museum of the mind, perhaps.

MARK: One of the things I was most intrigued about by your book is that even though you talk about McQueen and Westwood, and the exhibitions of their work that you curated, you never mention their names. You actually mention no designers apart from Old Town, the label made by Will Brown and Marie Willey at their workshop on the coast in Norfolk, whose work I know you wear a lot. Will Brown used to make clothes for David Bowie, and he was a big part of the London fashion scene, but nowadays Old Town is a fairly left-field artisanal operation. What's particularly fascinating about them is that they have employed fake memories in their work—they make garments that they say are "unfaithful" copies of pieces found in old lockers in locomotive works. Will calls it "fictitious provenance—an aid to the imagination." But it's just narrative. What's going on there?

CLAIRE: It is their sense of humor. And it is very English. But fashion is all about invention and reinvention, so why not? What I like about Old Town is that nothing is outsourced. You can hear the sound of shears cutting through cloth in the workrooms upstairs, the hiss of the iron, and the intermittent sound of a sewing machine, or Will's beloved buttonhole machine. But they don't make life easy for themselves—the way the clothing is constructed and the predominance of topstitching give the garments, and the wearer, nowhere to hide. They are uncompromising. When I discovered their clothing it was a relief, because I've always wanted the pressure taken off me, fashion-wise. I wear their clothes all the time. They don't change. I never have to get rid of them.

MARK: I am interested in designers who employ dead-stock fabrics and even weave textiles from processed old cloth. If you're using something from the past, what does that bring to the present garment, beyond circularity of production?

CLAIRE: I didn't realize when I was buying vintage in my twenties that it was generational. There seemed to be an inexhaustible supply of 1940s crepe dresses. I only realized later that those garments had come from women who had died, and that the supply was finite. That was then overlaid by the loss of another generation that released fashions from the 1950s into the market. But today, recently purchased clothing becomes vintage almost overnight and I worry that soon it will be specifically created for the pre-loved market. However, what's great about those designers using otherwise redundant fabrics—as well as Harris Reed, who is recycling old wedding dresses into ball gowns—is that repurposing fabric in this way is not just better for the planet but means the garments already have an inbuilt history. It gives them an additional resonance. But it's important to remember that this is not new. In the nineteenth century most woolen garments were recycled, "turned," and eventually shredded as part of the Shoddy trade, which is why there aren't many men's frock coats, for example, in museums. Recycling drove fashion. And it should do again. Just don't cut up vintage Schiaparelli.

1 | The Idiosyncratic Fashionistas

Valerie and Jean are a short story of the city: a chance encounter, a life-changing friendship, and the discovery of a shared goal. They met at a vintage show in New York in 2008. "Jean was wearing a great hat," says Valerie of the evening. "I am very shy, but I can talk to anybody who is wearing a hat." She invited Jean to the opening reception of her exhibition of antique Japanese children's kimonos at the Forbes Gallery, and the rest is social media history. They like to keep their professional backgrounds—entirely unrelated to fashion—distinct from what they do as the roving Idiosyncratic Fashionistas: recording, promoting, enabling, and generally cheerleading for mature women with an appreciation of innovative style. "We were corporate whores by day," says Jean. "Then we just kind of became ... the ladies that ran around."

In an era of growing conservatism in the city, particularly among the young, they are a breath of fresh air. Valerie and Jean are the epitome of local color in Manhattan and as much a part of "old New York" as a booth at Indochine and the bar at Raoul's. While they are familiar faces at parties, openings, and shows, there is a serious aspect to the Idiosyncratic Fashionistas: ageism remains abysmally and casually accepted in so many areas of the culture, despite a population increasingly dominated by people past retirement age. In a world that fears growing up and growing old, Valerie and Jean are an inspiration to women everywhere, of all ages.

Valerie (left) and Jean (right) in the 191st Street subway tunnel, New York.
Valerie wears a red puffer vest by The Eight Senses, coat by Heydari, and skirt by
Issey Miyake. Jean wears short Sleeping Bag Coat and turban by Norma Kamali,
quilted jacket by Ivan Grundahl, harem pants by Issey Miyake, peplum knitted top by
Mitsuhiro Matsuda, boots by Trippen, and felt pin by Danielle Gori-Montanelli.

MARK: Before we talked about you being a part of this project, I had seen you both out at events in New York for several years. It took me a while to get a handle on what it was you were doing beyond going to parties. The first time we spoke, you came up and asked to take a photograph of a pair of John Moore shoes I was wearing at the opening of the Antonio Lopez retrospective at El Museo del Barrio. You gave me your card, and I checked out your blog and thought, "Ah, this is something really interesting." It wasn't just about going to the cool thing that night, it was reaching out to a generation of older women and making a point about staying visible.

JEAN: Since I retired, I volunteer with the NY Senior Medicare Patrol and do a lot of outreach to seniors on how to avoid being scammed or a victim of identity theft. And what I've found is that even in a nursing home, ladies like to dress. It's about putting yourself together. You want to look your best, which helps you feel your best.

VALERIE: Our clothes are one of the reasons people noticed us when we first started hanging out together. In fact, it's one of the primary reasons we started the blog and then the Instagram. It's always interesting to me that we get nods of approval from everyone regardless of age, gender, ethnicity. A woman even asked me if I could be her professor instead of the one she had (though she didn't say for what subject ...). Lots of young people have told us that they had been afraid of getting old, and now they see it can be great fun. And they're right, it can be and is. I don't understand why people want to give up on expressing themselves visually as they age. Growing up in the 1960s, when we had Missoni, Rudi Gernreich, Mary Quant, and all those other exciting, brilliant designers, I just can't imagine waking up one morning, and saying, "Oh, I don't want to do that anymore, I'll just wear T-shirts and blue jeans."

JEAN: I think it might be peer pressure. If your group—say, your bridge club—looks a certain way, you get a little negativity if you start looking different, because it's threatening to them on some level. People want to blend in.

VALERIE: I was listening to Zac Posen in an interview today and he was saying that if he could change anything it would be "underdressing," because it's always better to be overdressed than underdressed. That has always been my mantra too.

MARK: The Idiosyncratic Fashionistas have a certain set of what I'd call "brand values." I love the way you work as a team, visually, but that you are also distinct entities within that. Where do you cross over in terms of your aesthetic, and where do you diverge?

JEAN: Valerie has many more pieces of clothing with color in them. I'm much more comfortable in black. Often when I wear color, it's out of guilt. I look in the wardrobe and think, "You know, I paid good money for this. I gotta wear it!"

VALERIE: Jean's right—it is hard to find good color and good color combinations these days. Bill Cunningham photographed me wearing a butter-yellow silk Armani pantsuit in the 1997 Easter Parade in New York. I wore that for a good ten years before I wore it out, and held on to it for another five. When I finally let go of it, I eulogized it on our blog. I still haven't been able to find a replacement for that, and I've been looking for years.

You know the olive Miyake suit that was on the cover of *Threads* magazine—it was called the origami suit, I think. I got that in the 1980s and wore it into the 1990s, till it was literally threadbare. I still have it rumpled up in my closet in case I ever decide to have it copied, but I haven't been able to find a new olive suit either.

I find bits of color here and there and incorporate them into my wardrobe as much as possible, but the unusual colors are hard to find. You can still get red and blue, but any other color is a tall order. Mustard is in this year, so I scooped up a couple of yellow shirts and yellow suede boots. I think color has disappeared because it's one more way brands can maximize profits. It's so irritating because color is such a great way to express yourself.

JEAN: Which is one of the reasons we buy vintage all the time. I don't shop in the big stores. I go to vintage shows rather than buy online. I have to see it and touch it. I must see if it gnaws at the back of my brain: "Buy me, buy me."

MARK: In terms of your personal collections, what are the oldest pieces you own that you bought new rather than acquiring as vintage?

JEAN: I have a pair of white Wrangler jeans, which I bought in 1963. I can't give them up, they're fabulous. They are solid white, with a tiny bit of red stitching right at the zipper. They're just the most utilitarian, perfectly designed garment. When I look at them, they take me straight back in time with more immediacy than a photo album ever could. They live in the bottom of an Amelia Earhart suitcase that I've been lugging around to different apartments for years.

I also have a Betsey Johnson Alley Cat sweater from 1972, and some Elio Fiorucci from the same year, bought before I moved to New York. I also have a lot of things from my mother, including a really neat plexiglass 1950s handbag. But that's not just any bag—it's the one that has little pieces of crumbled Kent cigarettes in the bottom because that's what she carried them around in, and a John Wayne business card, autographed, and something from one of the astronauts of the time, because she went to the Navy Ball every year. Movie stars and astronauts attended and danced with their wives, so it was a big deal. It's not a bag, it is someone's memories.

MARK: You mentioned Fiorucci—did you shop at the Fiorucci store, the mothership in Manhattan? It had closed before I started coming to New York in the second half of the 1980s, but it was so legendary from 1976 onwards, when Joey Arias worked there and there was a whole scene surrounding it. It was so much more than just a shop.

JEAN: I bought my first Fiorucci at the store in Washington D.C., but I definitely bought stuff from the Manhattan store when I moved to New York. I had a banana-yellow jumpsuit with a trim that would glow in the dark. If you stepped off a kerb at night in it, and you were caught in headlights, it was like "*Wow!*" It was great. The store itself was amazing, too, as you say, with Joey of course, and Patrick McDonald, who is such a dandy now, both working there.

VALERIE: The oldest thing I own that I bought myself is a pair of hot pants. We all had to embroider our own pants back in the day, and my brother suggested I put a train track and a tunnel on the back of mine. I was shocked. The prude in me thought the idea was just beyond the beyond, but then after a couple of days of ruminating on it, I thought, "Actually that's a really cool idea," so I did it. I wore the pants to school, with a bowler hat I'd been given at a concert by a really cute guy—a total stranger—because back then that was the kind of thing we all did. My French teacher, seeing me wear the hat, taught me how to say "chapeau melon."

MARK: So many of us throw away what we owned as teenagers, maybe as a rejection of what we were, or just because we aren't so sentimental at that age. What instinct made you keep those pants?

VALERIE: I'd worked so hard on them, and the embroidery came out pretty well, considering I didn't know what I was doing. I wasn't taught any handicrafts, so I kept them almost to prove to myself that I had the ability. Of course, I can't get into them anymore.

Another favorite that I can't bring myself to part with is a pair of wooden platform shoes with red leather T-bone straps that I bought in Italy when I did a semester abroad. I could never part with them even though I'd worry about breaking my ankles in them today.

Some of the earliest stuff that I still have is by Issey Miyake, from when I lived in Japan in the 1980s. It was the height of his extraordinary knits and wovens period, when his studio was trying all sorts of new and different things that just aren't done anymore. What Miyake does now with his pleats is interesting and innovative, but what he did back then was absolutely radical {page 42}. He was always coming out with something that made you wonder, "How did they do that?" or "What did they make that out of?" If the label detailed cloth that contained ten percent alpaca, I'd look to see if I could figure out which part that ten percent was. The warp? The weft? The trimming? I have held on to a lot of those pieces even though I seldom wear them.

MARK: I love that you mention Miyake and have that connection with the work. He was the very first designer I bought, when I was growing up in London. I went to his *Bodyworks* exhibition at the Boilerhouse Project—the precursor of the Design Museum—at the V&A in 1985 and was blown away by the forms. I bought pieces whenever I could afford them—double cotton shirts, jumpsuits, and T-shirts with extra panels at the back so they folded in a sculptural way. His work was so powerful.

JEAN: The first designers I bought were Betsey Johnson and Norma Kamali. Later on, I'd buy from Vivienne Tam. And Parachute when they had their store in SoHo. They had incredible pants and jumpsuits and things.

MARK: Parachute is a label that most people have forgotten about, but in the mid-1980s it was everything in New York, wasn't it? It was founded by Harry Parnass, an architect, and designer Nicola Pelly. It was pure rock star. It really embodied SoHo when it was a haven for the avant-garde. I always think of it as having a similar energy to Stephen Sprouse.

JEAN: What really made the Parachute store so great was the selection. The men's department was almost the same size as the women's, which was very unusual. They had lots of big-shoulder pieces, and of course a lot of the garments were made from parachute silk and nylon material. That was back when SoHo was SoHo, before it was all about Victoria's Secret on the corner and mall shops.

VALERIE: I remember getting a mini cape from Parachute. It had been $50, and they put it on sale for $25. I was fourteen, and I walked into the shop and I really wanted it. It just about made my eyes pop. I had babysitting money, but it was still a lot to me. I put a five-dollar deposit on that thing—it was all I had—and came back a week later to pay the rest and pick it up. It was the dead of winter, but I couldn't wait to wear it. It was too short to keep me warm, but I wore that cape like it was a mink coat.

MARK: Did you see those brands—Parachute, Betsey Johnson, and Norma Kamali—as being quintessentially New York? Or did you just see them as cool clothes?

JEAN: When I went home to D.C., I couldn't find them. Unless you went to Georgetown, but Georgetown just had a few boutiques, like Rich's Gaminerie. It was a big deal when they got a little Norma Kamali boutique. So yes, it was all linked to New York.

VALERIE: I didn't look at brand names. I looked at anything that was in direct opposition to the rather dreary, prissy period I grew up in. The stores that attracted me carried those brand names, so I was drawn to the stores more than the brands. I was too young to think that anything was "New York" or not, so I just saw them as cool.

MARK: And when did you both start getting interested in vintage?

VALERIE: Well, in the 1960s, vintage was cheap, accessible, and insouciant. And it had so much credibility. It was worn by people like Mick Jagger—there are some wonderful pictures of him wearing old velvet jackets from the 1930s. The designer Holly Harp was a big thing, too. She opened her first store in the 1960s in Los Angeles. I'm sure you've seen all the pictures of Janis Joplin wearing all her oddly matched stuff—fringes, chiffon, and bell bottoms. It was all in the spirit of vintage. That had been the kind of stuff that our parents threw away and didn't value anymore. There was a period where you could pick up Mariano Fortuny's Delphos gowns for nothing because most people didn't want to dress like it was the 1930s. They wanted to wear their miniskirts and show off their bodies. Vintage was cheap, but it was valuable to us, too, because although it wasn't new to our parents' eyes, it was new to ours.

JEAN: I probably got more interested in vintage in the 1980s. When I first moved to New York I lived on the Upper East Side, which was full of Wall Street banker types. Their dressing was preppy, totally preppy. I was preppy when I grew up in D.C.—my high school was full of people in saddle shoes and knee socks, and cardigan sweaters. Everyone wore Villager and John Meyer of Norwich and print dresses in the summer. Vintage didn't work in that crowd. I was always the one that dressed weirdly. I remember going out with somebody who picked me up for the evening and I was wearing a big red plaid circle skirt. He rolled his eyes and said, "Couldn't you just, for once, dress like everybody else?" I wasn't trying *not* to dress like everybody else—I was just wearing what I wanted to wear.

MARK: Jean, a lot of your style is about details and accessories, all your Bakelite bangles and other jewelry [**opposite**]. When did your passion for that begin?

JEAN: I always had it. My mother was a dresser. She was what they call a "clothes horse." My parents socialized a lot and my mother had a bridge club, and it was competitive dressing every evening. When you are playing bridge, your hands are always seen, so rings and bracelets are important. The Bakelite came from my grandmother, who owned a lot of it. When she died, my aunt and my uncle took some and my dad brought some home, which my mother thought was cheap, because she was more about diamonds. But I just thought it was the greatest thing in the world—the amber beads were so beautiful. I kept it all. Then I started collecting at flea markets and garage sales. I was in a summer house first in Connecticut, and then in the Hamptons, and on weekends you could go to a garage sale in those places and get a Bakelite bracelet for $5. The intricate hand-carved ones were maybe $25. And now you go to vintage shows, and they're like $250 and up, because of the demand.

MARK: That's an extraordinary hike. What happened to change that market?

Jean's vintage Bakelite bracelet collection: butterscotch and green bracelets *c.* 1930s; octagonal, faceted, and beveled bracelets *c.* early 1940s; ivory-colored bangles *c.* late 1940s.

VALERIE: There was just this one guy buying them. He was an accountant at a law firm, and he was embezzling millions of dollars from them. Eventually they caught up with him, but until they caught up with him, he was going to vintage shows and was buying Bakelite without even asking the price. The dealers got to know his taste, and because he had an endless supply of money, he drove the prices way up. Dealers loved him. When he was arrested the collection went to Doyle, the auction house. I went to see it and the selection was incredible. Everything in it went on to sell at an incredible price. Apparently, he also collected Bes-Ben hats. What I wouldn't give for one of those!

JEAN: It's a very specialized market now. People know the difference between celluloid and Bakelite, and that certain "green" Bakelite that doesn't have formaldehyde in it. The French used to make really cool carved, swirly things that looked very Egyptian. It's all so beautiful.

MARK: Let's talk about the clothing you treasure in your collections. The things that really mean most to you, for whatever reason.

JEAN: For me, it's a Greco-Roman dress by Norma Kamali with shoulder pads, cut with a big V down the front. It was so very 1980s, so of the moment. And it was just great. It was my wedding dress. My mother's whole bridge club came to New York for the ceremony, and I remember my mother took one of the flowers out of one of the arrangements, came over and stuck it in the front of my dress.

MARK: Was it white?

JEAN: It was! I was *Bride of Frankenstein*. I had my head shaved on the side, and it was gelled straight up, and I had lightning bolts dyed blonde platinum in my hair. My mother was not amused. I was thirty-six and all my girlfriends were married or on their second husbands at that point. I was like … "I'm gonna party!" We had it at Exit Art on West Broadway, which was a gorgeous open space with landscapes on the walls, but on the night of my reception the theme of the show was "overdose." There was one giant painting of a guy with his throat slit, drinking beer, and they had fake blood on the floor. It was right where my mother's table was supposed to be, so I said, "You have to move her table," because obviously we couldn't move the art. There was also a neon artwork in the back by Bruce Nauman, and it said "DEATH," and the D and H would blink on and off, so it would read "EAT DEATH … EAT DEATH." My 92-year-old aunt from Pennsylvania was there with my cousins, and three years later I was at a big family party and my aunt said: "You know, Jean, your wedding was the most fun wedding we ever had. I always say, what's a wedding without 'Eat Death'?" All my cousins burst out laughing. It was so funny. So that Norma Kamali piece is my absolute favorite dress, ever.

VALERIE: I am most fond of the Issey Miyake pieces that were designed by Junichi Arai and Makiko Minagawa. The amount of work and creativity that went into making them is just incredible. They really need to be seen close-up.

MARK: You are also still very active in buying and collecting new labels, aren't you? Like that red down coat by The Eight Senses that you wore for our shoot in the tunnel at the 191st Street Station [page 24].

VALERIE: The woman who designs them is called N. She's extremely creative and her work is full of loving detail. I'm very impressed with her way of thinking. That red coat is a technical marvel. The shape is simple—it's square, with two zippered arm holes—but it closes with magnets, so it's easy to work with, folds easily, and she's put a big zipper pocket in the seat, so the whole coat can be converted into a bag when I take it off. And I haven't done it yet, but I could use it as a comforter if I wanted to. It's stellar!

JEAN: I also love The Eight Senses. They often have good hidden pockets and really cool diagonal cuts.

MARK: When I first saw that coat, I thought it might be a Norma Kamali design I wasn't familiar with. It has that same sense of volume and use of materials.

VALERIE: I've had three Norma Kamali Sleeping Bag Coats [page 44], and I'll bet that's what attracted me to The Eight Senses puffer coats. Norma made a very early impact on me. I bought one of her dresses in Japan and wore that thing to death. Then I dyed it, but did a very bad job of it, so I got rid of it, but I kept the shoulder pads to reuse because they were so good. I also have her iconic black-and-red chequered dress with great big batwings. Once I had an amazing burgundy suede jumpsuit of hers. I very much regret giving that up now. I've never seen another one like it.

MARK: I am really interested to hear whether either of you were shopping at Charivari when it was around. It was such a landmark thing, and so influential. The family who ran it brought serious Japanese and European fashion to New York—Yohji, Issey Miyake, Armani, and Helmut Lang—when it still looked shocking. It was a part of the lexicon of 1980s high style in New York. Whenever you saw any interesting fashion in the shoots in Andy Warhol's *Interview* and checked the stockist details, it would always be "Available from Charivari."

JEAN: You had to really save your money to buy stuff there. It was in a price range that was up there. But you're right, they had designers that you wouldn't see anywhere else. Nowhere else. A lot of the crepe de chine stuff, a lot of the knits, incredible tailoring and cuts, and fabrics and things—all remarkable. And it wasn't like a big department store where they would have fifty of something. They'd have two or three in your size and that was it. They stocked Mugler, who was a designer that I absolutely loved. I would never see his clothes anywhere that I could possibly afford them. But they were so amazing, so beautiful. And the women that wore them, and the aura that he would create for his shows and things, with all those powerful women with these big shoulder pads ... They were Amazonian, tall and thin, with very sleek hair. There was nothing else like it.

VALERIE: That was before my time and before my budget. I have, to this day, one—count 'em, one—black Charivari sweater. I never see that label in second-hand stores.

MARK: Is there anything to compare to the likes of Charivari and Mugler now?

VALERIE: Maybe not. Not off the top of my head. It's hard for me to even define what the "in" look is today. We don't seem to have a zeitgeist unless it's jeans and T-shirts on the one hand, or over the top on the other hand. The looks of the 1960s and 1980s were very powerful and cohesive, but I don't see any power or cohesion in today's styles. And if there were a new look, I wonder if people would recognize it. If you look at fashion magazines now, nothing is presented in a way that makes you feel magnetically drawn to it, or that reveals its beauty and originality. Part of the problem is photography and layout, because the magazines now are all very cut and dried, very uniform. They just show things as product, without context.

MARK: And it's all "full looks" to please the advertiser, which kills the styling and creativity.

JEAN: I think there are places where you can still feel the magic. We like the Philadelphia Museum Craft Show, because they always have true craftspeople there, and you'll still find a sweater that is an unusual shape or fabric. I like Amy Nguyen, who does incredible shibori Japanese pieces, hand-dyed and hand-cut. She created one piece with a collection of triangles on what looks like netting, and when you hold it up to the light, the triangles show up while the netting becomes see-through. She makes exquisite things.

MARK: Do you think there are any inherently "New York" labels anymore? It's great that Norma Kamali is still doing what she is doing—and innovating, trying to get men to wear it—but it is difficult to think of others. I've seen you wear Maria Cornejo's work, Valerie, and I think she is really interesting—I remember her working with John Richmond as part of Richmond Cornejo in the mid-1980s in London, and they were contemporaries of BodyMap and Galliano. They were huge in their way, with stores all over Japan. Now Zero + Maria Cornejo is what I think of as totally New York, and quite unique because it's independently run so she does what she likes.

VALERIE: I love that Maria Cornejo dress—it has a pattern that is graffiti-like, reminiscent of Cy Twombly. I wear it back to front, because with the cut and shape, I don't think it matters and I prefer it that way.

MARK: I really like how you wear your pieces the way you want. You aren't dictated to by the designer and the garment.

JEAN: Thinking purely of designers based in New York, I think Yeohlee Teng is amazing. She is originally from Malaysia and does some interesting things with her conceptual, geometric silhouettes, which are great for women of a certain age with money. "Urban nomad" is how she describes her aesthetic. She manufactures in the city, and she's one of these people that is very adamant about keeping it local. She also advocates zero waste and I really respect that.

MARK: How do you feel being in New York influences the way you wear clothes today?

JEAN: Living here means I can actually wear all the stuff I buy. A friend of mine visited recently—she was here in the 1970s and 1980s but she moved to Santa Fe in the 1990s and got married, and she just said she doesn't dress out there because nobody else does. They dress casual. And we don't do that. We are never going to underdress.

Jean's pleated dress by
Issey Miyake *c.* 2011;
mesh top by Jean Paul
Gaultier *c.* 2010;
turban by Norma
Kamali, 2018.

Jean's reversible coat by Chunghie
Lee, 2011; jacket by Yoshiki
Hishinuma, *c.* 2008; harem pants by
k3 co.,ltd, *c.* 2010; hat by Ignatius
Creegan and Rod Givens, 2018.

Jean's coat by A
Tentative Atelier,
2017; sleeveless dress
by Issey Miyake Fête,
c. 2008; straw bowler
hat by Henrik Vibskov,
2015; collar (made
from scarf) and pin
cushion decoration by
Yayoi Kusama for
Uniqlo/MoMA, 2012.

Jean's coat, unsigned, *c.* 2017; top by
Junya Watanabe for Comme des
Garçons, *c.* 2012; high-waisted pants
by Donna Karan, *c.* 2010; bag by
Comme des Garçons, *c.* 2012;
necklace by Carol Cramer, 2014.

Jean's coat by Junya
Watanabe Comme des
Garçons x Puma, Spring/
Summer 2013; jacket by
Brigitte Vosse, 2012; shirt by
Sisley, *c.* 2015; pleated pants
by Issey Miyake, *c.* 2010;
vintage leather aviator
helmet, *c.* 1940s.

Valerie's printed pajamas
by Irregular Sleep Pattern,
2021; unsigned straw hat
from Japan.

41

Valerie's computer-woven top and skirt with 3-D embellishments by A-POC (Issey Miyake and Dai Fujiwara), Autumn/Winter 1999; hat by Schiaparelli, *c.* 1950s.

Valerie's sleeveless tunic, top and fishtail skirt by Pleats Please Issey Miyake, *c.* 2010; straw hat by Daniele Meucci, 1996.

Valerie's shibori Sleeping
Bag Coat by Norma
Kamali, Spring/Summer
1993; Persian lamb hat,
unsigned; hand-felted
scarf by Natalia
Shchirovskaya,
date unknown.

Valerie's balloon skirt by Issey Miyake Fête, *c.* 2011; jacket by Ivan Grundahl, *c.* 2011; halo crown, shoulders, and cage skirt with LED lights by Chromat, *c.* 2013; brooch with interchangeable parts from The Museum of Modern Art, New York, 2014.

45

2 | Charlie Casely-Hayford

The Casely-Hayford family has had a highly visible and powerful presence in British menswear for decades, mixing a streetwear sensibility with Savile Row codes. Influences and references include the youths of Kingsland Road between Dalston and Shoreditch, Ottoman and Wedgwood-inspired graphics, the biker boys of Seven Sisters, skinheads, and Sgt. Pepper. Garments have mixed crushed velvet and eveningwear with gray jersey sweats. An extensive archive includes collaborations with artist Chris Ofili and tailoring for The Clash and Lou Reed.

Joe Casely-Hayford OBE launched his first eponymous label in 1984 alongside his wife Maria. The pair met while studying at Saint Martin's School of Art in London. His first commercial collection was crafted from Second World War tents he discovered in a warehouse in Clink Street, and he went on to become one of the biggest design stars in London during the 1980s. After a successful period of designing directional womenswear and menswear, he focused on the latter. The Joe Casely-Hayford label was put to rest in 2006 when he took over as creative director at Gieves & Hawkes, before going on to launch the Casely-Hayford label with his son Charlie three years later. Joe Casely-Hayford passed away in 2019, aged sixty-two. The family business continues under the direction of Maria and Charlie Casely-Hayford.

Charlie Casely-Hayford on Ridley Road Market, London.
Suit by Casely-Hayford.

MARK: I'm interested to know how you feel about the Casely-Hayford archive when you look at it now. It's not just your work or your father's work—it's a family history.

CHARLIE: It's one of the few pure connections that I have with my dad. I go into the archive every season, and that's how I talk to him. When we were designing together, the conversation was the fundamental concept of the brand—a dialogue between father and son, with different perspectives on the same concept. I feel like I'm still able to do that by engaging with his work.

MARK: What was the dynamic between you when you were creating together?

CHARLIE: It developed while I was studying at the Courtauld Institute, and he was at Gieves & Hawkes. I started to feel like I had a valid enough sense of self to engage in a creative dialogue with him. And Dad was really into the idea of unlearning—he was so knowledgeable, he liked to step back and see things from a different perspective. Everyone always assumes that because I was the younger one I was bringing the more forward-thinking ideas to the table and it was Dad that brought the gravitas, but it was actually the other way around. It was a wonderful relationship. It's hard to describe how his mind worked, he moved so quickly.

MARK: How much of a physical archive is there? We are talking about an extraordinary and extensive body of work, incorporating his designs and then everything you created together.

CHARLIE: When my parents had their studio on Shoreditch High Street, about thirty years ago, they were able to maintain a fairly vast space for relatively little expenditure, so they kept everything. Me and my sister Alice used to spend a lot of time going into that archive, just looking around. We have vivid memories of it. Regrettably, they put a lot of pieces in sample sales in the late 1990s, because we moved and had less space. In hindsight, of course, we wish we hadn't done that, but we still have a significant number of pieces going back to before I was born.

MARK: Are there pieces in that archive that have a particular resonance for you?

CHARLIE: There is the shirt that you've shot for the book that has an extra panel at the front, which you can button up numerous different ways [**page 63**]. It was the design that sort of launched my dad's career in the 1980s. I have met so many people who tell me they had that shirt, and they still own it. A piece of clothing doesn't generally have that impact. They must have sold so many of them when they were first produced.

MARK: Would you ever bring it back as a reedition?

CHARLIE: We revisit one or two pieces each season, but I am scared to go near that one. It feels like it defined an era too strongly to revisit.

MARK: It's such a remarkable design. That shirt is similar to a lot of things Glenn Martens has done at Y/Project, and Martens has said that he wants his customer to be active in making decisions about how to wear his work. Your father's original shirt appeared around the same time that John Galliano was creating men's trousers with three legs. The idea was that you were supposed to tuck the leg into the fly—it sounds ridiculous, but the drapes and folds made it look superb. Clothes were about styling, and the garment itself didn't dictate to you. You had to work out how you wanted to wear them. You must hear a lot of stories about people obsessed with the early days of your dad's label.

CHARLIE: Every few days someone comes into the store and tells me they saved up their whole student loan to buy a single piece. I like to relive the experience of the original designs through their stories. Those people have an emotional connection with the clothes that doesn't happen with fashion now. Things are different.

MARK: Why don't we have that connection now? The avant-garde isn't dead, but it isn't the same.

CHARLIE: No, it's not dead, but there was a lot more engagement with the customer when my dad started. That way of thinking on the part of the customer doesn't exist on such a large scale now. People who come to Casely-Hayford now, who were customers in the past, are from diverse backgrounds. When you think of designers who are pushing boundaries today, their market is relatively niche. Until the 1990s the general public engaged with fashion on a deeper level.

MARK: What shifted that?

CHARLIE: It's impossible to say precisely, but certainly globalization has a lot to do with it. The currency of clothing isn't the same now. Brands and logos are far stronger than they ever were, and that has stifled creativity, as well as the way people engage with the actual clothing. The kind of man who wore the more experimental Joe Casely-Hayford pieces and went on to become an accountant doesn't exist now. Today, at Casely-Hayford, we design for people who have a certain confidence and who aren't consumed by logos. We aren't for everyone.

MARK: We seem to be seeing fashion diverge between understated luxury and product.

CHARLIE: There is now a chasm, which has been created by social media, and which doesn't feel sustainable. You have a collection of hype brands, and a lot of previously understated luxury brands are moving into that sector because it's profitable. I feel like a lot of founders of those labels would turn in their graves.

MARK: There are still holdout heritage brands. Hermès has collaborated with Leica and Rolls-Royce, but they operate in opposition to the hype brands.

CHARLIE: I'm not in any way comparing what we do to Hermès, but that is another family-run business that exists outside of the fashion cycle, which appeals to me and I respect. We are fortunate to have the foundations we do at Casely-Hayford because of what my dad did. Now I need to continue to tell that story. I know every designer says this, but I want people to buy our clothes and keep them forever. That was my dad's MO and it happened—people kept the clothes.

MARK: I've written about you and your father's work several times over the years, mostly for the *Financial Times*, and I was extremely honored and moved that he asked me to write his obituary while he was receiving palliative care at the start of 2019. It was shortly after your shop had opened on Chiltern Street in London, so it was yet another career high, but of course he knew he had terminal cancer. When he passed away, there was an outpouring of emotion from the fashion community that we'd never seen before. It's no understatement to say that he was truly beloved.

The obituary talks a lot about how his work could be subversive but always grounded in sartorial excellence. And I'd like to think it includes a summary of just how much he changed menswear during his career, which you're continuing to do:

> When Bono was the first man to appear on the cover of British *Vogue*, in 1992, he was wearing Joe Casely-Hayford. The construction of a Casely-Hayford suit is a feat of engineering—from the prominent chest with special internal darting to the prominent sleeve head roll, shaped sleeve with high underarm point and natural sloping shoulders. Casely-Hayford's design vocabulary incorporated lighter fabrics and ingenuity of cut to let the wearer move in ways tailoring hadn't allowed before, whether that was on the street, or on the stage. He deconstructed formal tailoring to create what he called 'new conservative dressing'. He was one of a handful of tailors—not just of his generation, but of the last 100 years—to push the boundaries of the medium and form, always creating something new, but always something that his loyal customer base, from New York to Tokyo, wanted to wear. He was grounded in being classless and cosmopolitan—he fashioned an ongoing document of the London in which he grew up and worked. When Joe passed away on 3rd January 2019 it was at the height of his influence and powers. The design world may have lost a gentleman and giant talent, and the Casely-Hayford family have lost a husband, father and friend, but his name and influence will live on.

Charlie Casely-Hayford on Ridley Road Market, London.
Suit by Casely-Hayford.

One of the things that we all think about when we think of Casely-Hayford is a family business. You are all very close, and Joe will forever be the bedrock of that. I'd love to hear about your earliest memories of your father, particularly in relation to the way he dressed. Like you today, he used his own clothes to illustrate just who he was.

CHARLIE: His style evolved. Sometimes he would show the most directional collection at Fashion Week and then come out himself dressed extremely formally in a suit. He was interested in playing with everyone's expectations of what a young Black designer should dress like. He didn't want to conform. But he was always sophisticated—whenever we went on holiday, most often to Italy, we would walk into a restaurant and you'd hear the clanging of cutlery as people turned to look at him. Even behind closed doors, he was immaculate the entire time. For a while he wore a totally crisp formal shirt to bed. Who was that for? It was just for him, no one else. He also dressed us when we were children. He made me a suit that was a replica of one from a collection he did, with displaced lapels, and had someone at Cordwainers make a tiny pair of brown leather boots to match.

MARK: Have many pieces from his personal wardrobe ended up archived?

CHARLIE: We have a lot. It was a real struggle to part of with any of it. He had a phenomenal shoe collection, over 100 pairs. He was a true connoisseur. And everything he owned was meticulous when he passed away. He wasn't necessarily about spending a lot of money on something, but he would put a shoe tree in a pair of Reebok Classics.

MARK: You mentioned people's preconceptions of what a Black designer should look like. We have to talk about this, of course. Casely-Hayford is a Black-owned company that has been around for a long time, yet still the rise of a Black-owned company like Telfar makes news. There also isn't a particularly long list of names of Black designers who have been successful in the past. There was Virgil Abloh, who was hugely inspiring to a generation. Willi Smith was lost to AIDS in 1987, aged thirty-nine, which was a huge tragedy. Patrick Kelly died at thirty-five, also lost to AIDS. Jay Jaxon worked in couture in the early 1970s but isn't as known as he should be. We have Grace Wales Bonner and Duro Olowu in London and Christopher John Rogers in New York, but the industry is still largely white. When I was working on a story for the *Financial Times* on the *Black Fashion Designers* exhibition at the Museum at FIT in 2016, I interviewed your dad about his perspective, and as he isn't here to represent himself, I'd like to include verbatim what he said:

> My work has been the reflection of a classless, cosmopolitan upbringing. I've more often had race imposed on my aesthetic than set out to create 'racial work'—growing up in London my influences have always been myriad. I've always occupied the same aesthetic ground—a place somewhere between English sartorial style and British anarchy.

My grandfather wrote a book called *Ethiopia Unbound*, its central theme being double consciousness and how a black man or immigrant can be fully conversant in an alien culture whilst retaining their other self. Although I am London-born, this concept has informed my creative process. My grandfather would wear his Ghanaian kente cloth while studying at Cambridge, and Savile Row suits in Accra. This action highlights his way of simultaneously functioning inside and outside of these two contrasting cultural boundaries.

I believe the term 'black designer' is sometimes used by the mainstream to refer to an outsider who is a lesser individual, who possibly operates within a different socio-economic structure.

Throughout my career I have worked to be defined by my output and not my color. There seems to be a lack of confidence in the ability of black designers, and the belief that black designers lack the positioning and social status to head up an international brand. I guess it's the sartorial equivalent of black pilot syndrome. I can say that for most of my career most people, even those working in fashion, would have struggled to name five black designers who show collections consistently on the European or international runways. It's positive to see this finally changing.

Your dad said he found that interview extremely uncomfortable at the time, and when we were emailing each other he always used "black" not "Black," but he understood how important the FIT show was.

CHARLIE: Whatever he did, whatever boundaries he broke, he was always defined by his race. It was always the label used, as if he could only ever be the best Black designer. I am very proud of who I am and where I come from, but that's not all that I am. It was the same with dad. From his perspective, that was all that was seen by the media. His intention was to show that he would not be defined by those labels. He pushed through. The media had already put so much emphasis on it, he didn't need to.

MARK: When we saw Black Lives Matter happen in 2020, it was interesting to see the industry try to make Black faces more visible in the media when not many Black people actually occupy senior creative or directorial positions. So suddenly we had a lot of Black models on the covers of magazines.

CHARLIE: It highlighted how lacking the industry is. My dad was wary, early in his career, of being described just as a Black designer, because the term came with a complicit narrowing, a complicit confinement. What he and his peers sought to do was to expand the language, expand the landscape of what Blackness and simultaneously Britishness meant and could mean. Even a single generation before him, my grandad's experience of Blackness was so clearly defined in its parameters by those who were non-Black. It was incredibly limiting and singular in its lack of understanding.

The intention has always been to open up the dialogue, communicate the complexities of what it is to be Black and British, but the fashion industry has quite often avoided the different categories of a Black person. Even later in his career, a lot of journalists struggled to comprehend the complexity of my father's intentions and how he chose to define himself. Every article I read through the 1980s and 1990s would lazily call him "London's best up and coming Black designer." He was up and coming for twenty years.

So, in 2020 the landscape was forced to change. People of color have been slowly given visibility at the front of the industry, even if it has often felt like tokenism. For me, it has always been about what's happening behind the curtain—that's where the problem needs to be solved. If you're not allowing people of color and minority groups the opportunity to at least earn their seat at the table in certain conversations and in the decision-making process, diversity is simply a box-ticking exercise and nothing more. This means everything from the classroom at art schools and business schools to the boardroom at the top level. The recent shift in culture is now allowing us to have these conversations. It feels like a very exciting moment. I often find myself wondering, if my six-year-old daughter were to continue the family business, what this evolving landscape might look like for her.

MARK: When did you first understand what your dad was doing and how important he was?

CHARLIE: I have vivid memories of him at his desk, and you couldn't see any of the surface of it because it was covered with sketches. The space behind him was stacked floor to ceiling with vinyl, and he picked out different music to inspire him every day. My strongest memory is of him sketching constantly, at the desk or at home. Then I remember the whole family going to see his show at London Fashion Week, and we were bumped from the first row to the second, because Princess Diana turned up.

MARK: That's a major memory for me too. It was the Autumn/Winter 1995 show. I didn't know you were there, but I was sitting on the floor close to you with my camera, at the end of the catwalk, waiting to shoot the show. Everyone became hysterical when she walked in. She was the most famous person on the planet. I've never seen the mood in a room change so quickly. The security started to shout at us all to turn back to face the catwalk so they could start the show.

CHARLIE: It was the first show she had ever been to, I believe. I was around nine years old. The next day it was on the front page of the *Evening Standard*, and my friends were all looking at it at school, and that's when I realized what it was my dad was doing. Up until then, it was hard for me to explain to my friends, because it was just clothes that they couldn't understand, with shirts that didn't button up in a normal way.

MARK: That was a significant moment as well because it represented the establishment endorsing British fashion, which had a reputation for being anti-establishment.

CHARLIE: I remember when my dad went to take over at Gieves & Hawkes. It was originally just a consultancy role and then Robert Gieve, who was the last generation of the founders to be there, made him Creative Director. They launched Gieves as a stand-alone label and took it to Paris in 2006. I remember going to that show and sitting right next to my dad and shedding a tear, because I knew he had cracked the most established of brands. He had gone from making clothes from Second World War tents in the 1980s to the most famous house on Savile Row.

Men's inside/outside gray striped jacket with embroidered contrast panels and Viyella shirt by Joe Casely-Hayford, Spring/Summer 1993; men's Caro outside seam striped trousers by Casely-Hayford, Autumn/Winter 2017.

Women's single-button jacket in navy plaid worsted with gray Prince of Wales check printed panels by Joe Casely-Hayford, Spring/Summer 1998.

Women's twisted leaf lapel jacket in brown linen and cream velvet raglan neck blouse by Joe Casely-Hayford, Spring/Summer 1990.

Men's double-breasted jacket in diamond
jacquard needlecord by Joe Casely-Hayford,
Autumn/Winter 1996; high-waisted
Bolero trousers in fine navy stripe
worsted by Joe Casely-Hayford,
Spring/Summer 1988.

Single-breasted Stonebridge coat/jacket hybrid in charcoal mélange wool by Casely-Hayford, Autumn/Winter 2014; Benson elongated hoodie in pale gray marl fleece by Casely-Hayford, Autumn/Winter 2015; gray textured cotton Basalto trousers by Casely-Hayford, Spring/Summer 2015; men's brogues by J.M. Weston for Casely-Hayford, Autumn/Winter 2014.

Men's 3-D lapel jacket in navy fine wool with taupe contrast at lapel by Joe Casely-Hayford, Spring/Summer 1991; men's cream silk shirt by Joe Casely-Hayford, Autumn/Winter 1989; men's Caro outside seam striped trousers by Casely-Hayford, Autumn/Winter 2017.

[Opposite]
Men's gray worsted
Japanese tailored,
semi-handmade jacket
and trousers by
Casely-Hayford,
Autumn/Winter 2009.

Men's Rules pale gray
worsted suit with dropped
hem by Casely-Hayford,
Autumn/Winter 2009;
unisex Off-The-Shoulder
white cotton shirt by
Joe Casely-Hayford,
Autumn/Winter 1985.

Coat (in collaboration with
Mackintosh) and women's
bouclé knit wool cardigan
with woven collar and
placket, by Joe Casely-
Hayford from *Supertramp*
collection, Autumn/Winter
2001; men's cream/claret
city stripe shirt with
asymmetrical fastening by
Joe Casely-Hayford,
Autumn/Winter 1986;
Straight 'N Narrow
trousers with hand-stitched
embroidery by
Joe Casely-Hayford,
Autumn/Winter 1998.

64

Women's green velvet jacket with red contrast castellated hem and wide-legged trousers in olive mélange wool with green velvet castellated hem by Joe Casely-Hayford, Autumn/Winter 1989; men's Club Boy shirt in cream silk with black club appliqué motifs by Joe Casely-Hayford, Autumn/Winter 1989; women's black suede, snout-toed shoes with red gloss heel by Joe Casely-Hayford, Autumn/Winter 2000.

3 | John Matheson – McQueen Vault

The full potential of social media as an open resource of fashion archives for analysis and research remains in its infancy. With few credible exceptions, the phenomenon of "the influencer" has led to backlash and ridicule, but the rise of John Matheson's McQueen Vault Instagram account (@McQueen_Vault) has shown how much potential digital platforms still have. Launched in 2018 as a part-time project by Matheson and his husband to showcase their obsession with the work of Lee Alexander McQueen, it rapidly attracted over 150,000 followers. When Matheson posts, a single image can receive over 15,000 likes.

Social media is fickle, and easy to dismiss as a serious tool for academics, but a community has grown around McQueen Vault, incorporating individuals who were peers and part of the designer's career and a younger generation who are discovering the work for the first time. The archive consists of edited videos, close-up details of garments, press clippings, and rarely seen photoshoots dating back to McQueen's graduate collection from Central Saint Martins in 1992 through to his suicide in 2010. Matheson's account has benefited from a steady flow of contributions from people keen to share their personal archive material, but its bedrock is Matheson's fascination with his chosen subject. Unlike any of the monographs that have been published on the late designer, McQueen Vault is a project that is developing and growing and has generated a dialogue with the international fashion and art community.

Matheson and his husband Pablo live in London and share a substantial personal archive of McQueen runway pieces, as well as a notable collection of Jean Paul Gaultier menswear.

John Matheson at Christ Church Spitalfields, London.
Jeans by Levi's; jacket by COS; boots by Dr. Martens.

MARK: You discovered Lee McQueen around the same time as a lot of people and the press, with the *Dante* show that he staged at Christ Church in Spitalfields, in March 1996. I was there taking photographs and you were watching it on TV in South Carolina. It's still the most powerful fashion show I've ever seen.

JOHN: When I saw that show it was like when you flip channels to the news and there is something jarring on screen, and a new kind of reality has landed. Everything about that production—the soundtrack of LL Cool J, *Adagio for Strings*, Gregorian chant, the Rolling Stones and gunshots, and the styling using imagery from Joel-Peter Witkin—spoke to me as a young gay man in the middle of Nowheresville, USA. It told a story about war and politics and religion. I fell passionately in love with what he was doing.

MARK: I had an almost identical experience a few years earlier. The first time I encountered his work was when MTV showed a montage of clips from the 1994 *Nihilism* show at Bluebird Garage in Chelsea. It was only about fifteen seconds of airtime but it was so aggressive, it was like a visual assault. I hadn't seen anything like it in fashion for years. Then I went to the Autumn/Winter show that same year, *Banshee*, at the Café de Paris, and I knew he was going to be the biggest star in fashion we had seen in a long time. Now it looks like he will be the last self-made fashion superstar because the industry is so different now. You can't start a label in the way he did. He was so focused and would stop at nothing to make it happen. There was the shock of the new, and people also really wanted to feel something shocking.

JOHN: I remember the moment in the *Dante* show when Kristen McMenamy walked down the aisle of the church in a slashed brocade jacket and, as I was looking at the Simon Ungless prints using Don McCullin's Vietnam War photography, questioning what I was watching and why I was so drawn to it. What was going on? How was this being done with clothing? Watching it again later, when I had a more refined appreciation for the intricacies and content, it made more sense. That show holds a special place for me. It was a gateway moment and summed up everything McQueen was about.

MARK: He was a true original and a lot of the press—apart from Issy Blow, of course—didn't know how to react. I was the first journalist to interview him for print, for a gay newspaper. I did it at his birthday party at Maison Bertaux, a few days after the *Banshee* show. There was always a touch of the savant about him—when I asked him what he had to say about accusations of his work being misogynist, he asked me to turn the tape recorder off for a moment so I could explain what the term meant.

He absolutely wasn't misogynist, of course—he loved women. He explained he liked to work with lesbian models because they were always candid about what he designed for a woman's body, and what turned them on. He said that the journalist who had called him a misogynist was "a stupid old queen who can go and fuck himself." Which was so Lee.

A couple of years later I took him to lunch at Nicole Farhi's restaurant, with someone I knew from Amex, because they wanted to get involved with his shows. Although, notoriously, they didn't go for *Golden Shower* as a title for the 1998 show with the water-filled catwalk and rainfall that Simon Costin art directed, so the invite read *Untitled*.

Lee and I eventually fell out, and I didn't really speak to him after he went to Givenchy. But that happened with a lot of people around him at the time. He was laser-focused on being a star.

JOHN: I saw him as someone who wasn't supposed to be in the system, but was, and poisoned it for the good. He was saying honest things, and not just being courteous to get ahead. He wasn't just being spiky; he had the talent to back it up. Every person I have met who worked with him speaks of him with respect and says he didn't just talk the talk—he could back it up with his own scissors. He had true technique and skill. Those show pieces are heirlooms and his samples are quite emotional. There are so many stories attached to them.

MARK: What you're doing with McQueen Vault is also storytelling, through ephemera and coverage linked to those shows. What have been some of the most surprising and exciting things you've come across?

JOHN: Well, the thing I really geek out on is the historical documentation, which is rare. Occasionally you see catalogues and invitations, but there are very few around. I bought one of the invitations for *Nihilism* (Spring/Summer 1994) from someone who was an associate of Lee's, which I think might be the only one in existence. I also have two original drawings. They are from around the time of *The Hunger* (Spring/Summer 1996), and you can tell from the sketches that he is working out ideas for sleeves and lapels. There's an amazing, almost hourglass-shaped cutout that comes together with a single button aligned with the inner elbow as part of a long frock coat.

MARK: Tell me about the actual clothes you own. How big is the collection and what are your most cherished pieces?

JOHN: My collection is best described as "reading between the lines." I collect out of curiosity and needing to see the detail and choices that have been made to execute a story. Along with a huge archive of documents and media, there are dozens of tailored garments, dresses, shoes, and accessories. I own some haute couture from his time at Givenchy, and many ready-to-wear pieces.

It particularly fascinates me to see his working process, and his team's—there's clearly an evolution of progress, change, and learning, including some missteps. I have a few original show pieces and working prototypes that illustrate these unique moments beautifully.

MARK: What are the standout collections and shows for you?

JOHN: There are so many, but I've been looking at *The Horn of Plenty* from 2009 a lot recently {page 85}. People say they love it because it's so gothic, but I think it's full of humor. There are a lot of jokes in there that people miss. He was poking fun at consumption and the tropes of couture at Chanel and Dior. The styling is over the top, and there's an insanity to the whole thing. John Gosling of Psychic TV, who also released his own music as Mekon, assembled a soundtrack from all the other previous show soundtracks, so it wasn't just about the trash pile in the middle of the show being pieces from previous show props, it was the soundscape too. There were 1990s club bangers playing, and all those insane-looking models walking around with this Elizabethan/Leigh Bowery/Catherine Deneuve-in-*The Hunger* make-up. It was a defining collection because you see everything come together perfectly—the wickedness, the romance, and the sense of humor. Visually it's pure fashion, but when you peel back the layers, it's deep and emotive. It was flawlessly executed. It's a much bigger show than people think. And there were always so many sensations he played on, like having Simon Costin blind the audience with giant lights as they walked into Borough Market for *It's a Jungle Out There* in 1997, and the smell and sound of the shingle on the catwalk at *Eshu* in 2000.

MARK: It's interesting you picked *Horn of Plenty*, and what you say about it. I was talking recently to someone who had been close to Lee and who worked with him at the start, but at the time of *Horn of Plenty* they hadn't seen him in a few years. When they went backstage at that show in Paris, they said he was in a horribly dark place, and it was really upsetting to witness. I wonder if his best work came from despair. It's often the way with artists.

JOHN: I think it came from myriad places, but for him that might have been his sweet spot, creatively. I actively avoid putting anything on McQueen Vault about his personal life. It's not my story. I have been told a lot of things in confidence, but I am a spectator in all of this. It doesn't feel right to repeat anything. What I will say is that knowing what we know now about mental health issues, and how awful the fashion industry can be, it can make people do shitty things.

Tension is what created a lot of the key moments in McQueen's career. *The Bone Collector* menswear collection from 2010, the year he died, is hard to watch for me because it was referencing stories from the old Irish whaling communities and the idea of loved ones going to sea, possibly never to return. The rope and chainmail photo-printed fabrics referencing lover's knots and all the mythology connected to what they represent to sailors leaves a lump in my throat.

MARK: He talked a lot about leaving fashion, but he seemed trapped by the whole thing. In October 2009 he showed *Plato's Atlantis*, which was an escapist fantasy, full of color, about his dream world, mixed with digital futurism. He always said he loved to dive and that he felt happiest beneath the surface of the water, with all the radiant sea creatures. It's particularly sad that he put that together while he must have been thinking about ending things.

John Matheson at Christ Church Spitalfields, London.
Jeans by Levi's; jacket by COS; boots by Dr. Martens.

JOHN: It was like a last burst of life.

MARK: Obviously Alexander McQueen the label remains a big business employing a lot of people, and the Sarabande Foundation that carries on in his name supports great talent, but Lee had such a strong personal vision, and we don't have that anymore. It's impossible to know what he would have done if he had still been around. Some brands transcend their founders and roots. Cristóbal Balenciaga closed the doors of his house in 1968 and died in 1972, and nothing was produced in that name until a revival in 1986. Some of Demna Gvasalia's couture at Balenciaga is a radical and brilliant update of the original ideas, but we're talking about fifty years of space that exists, so the concept of what Balenciaga is has become abstract. It can live on just as a name on a T-shirt. It's a brand. But with McQueen— and Gaultier, too—we're looking at recently active auteurs, and labels where there has been no real pause in production. It's weird to see guest designers like Sacai, Haider Ackermann, and Glenn Martens creating under the Gaultier umbrella, as amazing as the work might be. It's a bit like when John Galliano was removed from his own label, although that was effectively an eviction. Do you see the McQueen label after Lee's death as canon, or do you see the body of work he created personally as a completed act?

JOHN: *Angels and Demons* (Autumn/Winter 2010), which he was still working on when he died, and which was completed by the studio and shown posthumously, was an ideal bookend because it referenced many things from the past, but it was totally contemporary because of his use of technology and continuation of digital printing and pattern design. I still can't wrap my head around some of the fabrics and how they manipulated prints taken from medieval art and engineered them into brocades. These elements were pushed even further by using the brocades and prints to mirror anatomy and create trompe l'oeil effects on the body.

In terms of people stepping in to take over, I struggle with the idea that the fashion industry model is about creating a huge business empire. Alaïa was able to do something succinct and specific, and it was still desirable and successful, but it wasn't on sale in every shop—although that's now changing. I wish something like that could have been considered for McQueen, so it just became a niche British brand that delivered on its heritage. I was a big champion of Sarah Burton's work for quite a while, and then I felt it took a turn. There were ranges of sneakers coming out, and it felt like the tower was crumbling. I was in La Samaritaine in Paris recently, and the only sign of the brand was a solitary display of garish trainers and jumpers with logos on them. I was just sad. Will future generations even know what made the McQueen name important?

I don't feature much of the current brand on McQueen Vault, because the brand has its own social media, and I don't want to try and compete with that. I'm interested in a different era and the earlier stories.

MARK: There are now bum bags with McQueen scrawled across them. Burton is a great designer, but there are some abysmal things attributed to the McQueen name. They could have scaled it down and used the archive more. I don't understand why more designers don't focus on reeditions. You don't need to totally redesign the product every six months and tell a whole new story.

JOHN: I talk about this a lot in regard to Jean Paul Gaultier with my husband Pablo, who has a lot of his menswear. When Gaultier was still designing, he always told a big story every season, and we wondered why he didn't just go back to the archives and rerelease things. When you have a history that has had such an impact, and influenced pop culture so much, you don't need to come up with new product all the time.

MARK: There are so many older designs that people would buy instantly. The men's coats from *Dante*, for instance [page 80]. And when you think of Gaultier, all the tailoring from the 1993 *Chic Rabbis* collection, including the jacket that Pablo owns [page x]. Yohji does his Replica series of items remade from old patterns, but it's not something that's done enough. Bring back John Galliano's 1980s menswear, and Westwood and McLaren's Nostalgia of Mud! It shouldn't just be on 1stDibs for £10,000. Which is also what we're seeing with the market for early McQueen. And some of it is disingenuously marketed as a one-off runway piece, and we know that's not the case, because we know people who can verify it.

JOHN: People are bloodthirsty for those original show pieces from the early 1990s. I stumbled into all this and found pieces for reasonable prices online. But now there's a perfect storm with the resale market, and people are putting pieces up for sale at prices they know are unachievable, just to make their overall offering look high end. Recently, there was a beaded dress from McQueen's *Joan* collection in 1998 that sold for about $4,000, and then the next buyer put it on sale on a premium website for around $70,000. You also have celebrities buying things, which drives the price up, and other people buying them to copy, so there is layer upon layer that affects the pricing.

I don't want what I'm doing with the Vault to be a tool for people who work in the market to just use it for resale and add an extra digit to their prices. But I also can't help but do the research. It is a compulsion. I get excited when I see a poem on a couture dress from Lee's time at Givenchy, and I have to work out where the poem is from. And I will never stop collecting a physical archive. But what I look for is different from most collectors—I may buy a fabric swatch or garment when I can't see something clearly in pictures. *The Horn of Plenty* is a good example—there is a model's skirt that looks dipped quite simply in tar, but actually it is a whole scene painted in the style of Victorian silhouettes. You can't see that unless you have the garment in front of you, because it's printed on magnified houndstooth check. Discovering things like that is what keeps me coming back for more.

MARK: Lee was quite precious about the clothes and who they went to. A close mutual friend had a lot of pieces and was going to auction them in the early 2000s, and Lee gave him the cash equivalent on the understanding he wouldn't do that. But the pieces ended up ruined. He was a club kid who wore them out constantly.

I had a one-off coat I had borrowed for a shoot, which I kept hanging on my wall for a year because I loved it as an object. It was made from a kind of industrial plastic textile that Simon Ungless told me was something they found in a building supply warehouse. I felt bad that I'd kept it disingenuously, so I gave it back to Lee. He'd forgotten all about it, of course, and gave it to the friend I mentioned, who then decided to "restyle" it by ripping the sleeves off. It would be priceless now, but it's gone, like a lot of the early stuff.

It's also hilarious to think back to how feted Lee was in the early days in the style press. Everything would be credited as "Available from Pellicano in London," but as far as I know, they never had anything you could buy—it was only Issy Blow and a few friends and models who had any of the clothes. It's funny to see some of those tear sheets appear on McQueen Vault. I see that period of his career, when you couldn't actually buy anything, as fascinating. It was mythmaking. Even in 1996, with *The Hunger* and *Dante*, which had gone into production, it was hard to get hold of anything unless he was making it for you.

JOHN: I think it is easy to break up McQueen's career into three eras: the early work, the Givenchy era, and then the time after the investment from Gucci where it becomes a brand. You can see along the way how he had more and more access to resources. But it was always inspired. You can see subtle details at *Banshee*, when there's no budget, like a certain nip on a shoulder detail, and it's incredibly special. He also pulled together a universe around him, of all the right people—Katy England, Andrew Groves, Simon Costin, Shaun Leane, and Sarah Harmarnee—and it made it all come together. Then he went to Givenchy and stumbled, but good things came from those mistakes. He was experimenting with the ateliers and couture.

MARK: He didn't know what was possible at Givenchy at first. He sprayed things gold, as he had in London. Because that's what he knew, that's what he was doing in London. And of course, you don't do that with couture, you use actual gold thread. But he was irreverent and anarchic. He made it up as he went along.

JOHN: It was refreshing for that to happen in a couture house, for someone to find their way. When you get to his final era, with the digital printing and a bigger focus on accessories, the total picture became different. I mean, the Pepper's Ghost apparition of Kate Moss at the end of *Widows of Culloden* (Autumn/Winter 2006) was mid-nineteenth-century trickery absolutely made for a McQueen show. It was so beautiful—no wonder people were crying. I cried myself, too, when I saw it at the V&A *Savage Beauty* exhibition. Emotion may be tossed around in fashion as a buzzword, but McQueen delivered true emotion in spades. I can't think of another designer who had such a personal journey that was so public, and perhaps this is one of the reasons it was raw and sometimes rough—but it was always real. I watch the shows repeatedly and never tire of looking for new details. I fall in love with things over and over again based on the power of each show. They are an enduring mark of true genius.

Waxed linen wing-shoulder frock coat with rear illusion panel and wool cropped S-Bend trousers by Alexander McQueen, *No. 13* collection, Spring/Summer 1999.

Felted wool jigsaw-cut
long coat and pink
overdyed denim Bumsters
by Alexander McQueen,
The Overlook collection,
Autumn/Winter 1999.

Stamped leather multicolored karung Belt shoe with resin horn heel by Alexander McQueen, *Irere* collection, Spring/Summer 2003.

Men's charcoal solid
wool and pinstriped
peak lapel double
layered blazer by
Alexander McQueen,
Dante collection,
Autumn/Winter 1996.

Rose pebbled Donegal tweed
tie lapel suit and leather
trompe l'oeil curved heel
thigh-high boots by
Alexander McQueen,
Pantheon ad Lucem collection,
Autumn/Winter 2004.

Gradient gray wool and sharkskin paneled suit with pagoda shoulders and lace illusion back panel by Alexander McQueen for Givenchy Couture, *Blade Runner* collection, Autumn/Winter 1998.

Tibetan brocade croquet dress and
black studded leather tieback
knee boots by Alexander
McQueen, *Scanners* collection,
Autumn/Winter 2003.

Houndstooth ensemble with high-collar peplum jacket and circle skirt, photo-printed tie-neck houndstooth silk blouse, houndstooth knit tights, black kid leather opera gloves, houndstooth printed sunglasses and elevated houndstooth Correspondent pumps, all by Alexander McQueen, *The Horn of Plenty* collection, Autumn/Winter 2009.

4 | Sandy Powell

Few figures in the world of design have commuted between counterculture and establishment with the skill and success that Sandy Powell has. Even fewer are as visually striking as the work they produce. Well known for working regularly with directors Todd Haynes and Martin Scorsese, Powell has also created the wardrobes for a series of contemporary live action Disney blockbusters, putting Cinderella in state-of-the-art crystal heels that pushed the boundaries of technology at Swarovski, and refreshing *Mary Poppins* with a wardrobe inspired by the work of the nineteenth-century painter James Tissot.

Born, raised, and still based in South London, at the time of writing she has been nominated for the Oscar for Best Costume Design, and the BAFTA equivalent, fifteen times by each Academy. She started her film career in the 1980s creating costumes for queer filmmaker Derek Jarman, while also working on numerous live contemporary dance productions for choreographer Lea Anderson. She has won three Academy Awards, for *Shakespeare in Love* (1998), *The Aviator* (2004), and *The Young Victoria* (2009), and three BAFTAs, for *Velvet Goldmine* (1998), *The Young Victoria*, and *The Favourite* (2018).

In 2023, Sandy made history as the first costume designer to receive BAFTA's highest honor of a Fellowship.

Sandy Powell at Christopher's, London.
Suit designed by Sandy Powell and made by Ian Frazer Wallace, 2016.

MARK: Your job is to create characters intrinsic to the narrative of a film. Are you also creating a narrative and character yourself? Every aspect of your image has always seemed so considered.

SANDY: I don't think so. When I'm working on a film, I define a character by what they wear. I have to get into that character's head and figure out what they would choose and why. I don't do that with myself. Having said that, I have dressed in a certain way for a situation. At the start of my career, I used to wear what I thought of as my "lucky outfit," the Gaultier bomber jacket and black nylon leggings that you photographed [**page 102**]. I'm not superstitious—it just made me feel confident. There are times when clothing needs to be armor, but when I dress with that in mind, I don't feel like I am dressing out of character. Around about the same time I was wearing that Gaultier outfit, I wore a lot by Val Piriou, who was a designer from France who won Designer of the Year in London in 1990 [**pages 103–104**]. She died of AIDS in 1995 at thirty-one. Tragic.

MARK: When did the orange hair begin?

SANDY: I was fourteen. Henna hair dye color was the only thing I could afford when I went into the original Biba on Kensington High Street, although I then went on to shoplift makeup in Big Biba (sorry, Barbara Hulanicki!) when I was about sixteen. I've had unnatural hair color ever since. It just feels right to me when the alternative is mouse brown.

MARK: There are so many interesting things going on in fashion in terms of gender. When you wear a suit, is that you playing with the idea of gendered clothing? A woman wearing an oversized blazer suggests an inherent confidence, because women's clothing isn't grounded in the measurements and precision of tailoring, but there are still lingering conventions that dictate how men's clothing should look (unless we're talking about the supersized mainstream of streetwear). I still see suits as inherently masculine because of the expectation of precision of fit and cut.

SANDY: I've always worn suits, going right back to the 1980s. I don't see it as gendered. I wear dresses, but I'm much more comfortable in something tailored as opposed to pretty or "feminine." I'm not doing it to get noticed, it just makes me feel confident, and I know that it looks good.

MARK: I remember Bryan Ferry saying in an interview once that in the early days of Roxy Music he pretty much only wore his Antony Price suits, because he knew that in the future a suit wouldn't look old-fashioned in photographs, whereas anything that was "fashion" would look dated. You're now known for wearing a certain cut of suit from that same era, the early 1970s, but you've made it your own, and it looks totally contemporary, which in a way proves his point.

SANDY: I had that first suit made for me in 2015 by Ian Frazer Wallace who I have worked a lot with at the Whitechapel Workhouse. I wanted a perfect copy of the pale blue suit that Freddie Burretti made for David Bowie for the "Life on Mars" video in 1971. That Mick Rock video sums up so much for me. It's such a gorgeous image, so ingrained on my memory—the white background, the orange of his hair, blue eye makeup, and pink lips. I wanted to have a version of that suit made for me, and I knew I could get the cut perfect, but I couldn't find the right blue fabric. Then I was on a job in LA, had a spare half an hour to go to a textile shop, and there it was on the top shelf—just enough for what I needed. I've now had a batch of suits made from the same block. Some of the details are different, but it's always the same shape.

MARK: That blue suit is now as synonymous with you as it is with Bowie, and of course the calico toile Signature Suit, with the 200 film industry autographs on it, has become as famous [page 96]. It went straight from our shoot to the V&A. How did the idea come about?

SANDY: I was asked to pose for a portrait for BAFTA, and they wanted me shot in a workroom. I thought about making it more interesting by wearing a toile, and I realized that one of the suits looked really good. It was also a blank canvas. Awards season was coming up, I had been nominated for both a BAFTA and Academy Award for work on *The Irishman* (2019), and the Art Fund campaign to buy Prospect Cottage, Derek Jarman's home in Dungeness, had just started. It felt like prophecy. A lot of us who were involved with Derek had talked about how we could raise awareness and donations, and it seemed like such an obvious idea: wear the calico suit to events, get celebrities to sign it, and sell it. It also meant I didn't have to think about what I was going to wear all season. Robert De Niro and Al Pacino are on the lapels, Donatella Versace is on the back. There's Scarlett Johansson, Brad Pitt, Renée Zellweger, Leonardo DiCaprio, Elton John, Joaquin Phoenix, and Laura Dern. It sold for £20,000 at Phillips, the individual who bought it then donated it to the permanent collection at the V&A, and the Art Fund hit their target of £3.5m to protect Prospect Cottage and support future residency programs there.

MARK: You've also worn full-on glam red-carpet dresses to the Oscars. We photographed the gown you wore when you won the award for *The Aviator*, which is the same dress Cate Blanchett wears in the film, with the identical Art Deco pattern, but in a different color [page 101]. How do you feel in a dress in that kind of situation, as opposed to a suit?

SANDY: Usually freezing and exposed. You're on that red carpet with bare arms, and then you're inside and it is brutally air conditioned, so you're cold, but you're also sweating because you're nervous. It's a horrible combination. Also, you have to wear heels unless the dress is long enough to cover flats, and after a couple of hours it's agony.

MARK: You've clearly always known the power of clothes and use that skillfully. The first time you came to what we might consider the general public's attention was at the *Evening Standard* Film Awards in 1992. You won an award, partly for your work creating the costumes for Jarman's *Edward II*. I remember watching that ceremony on TV, at home with my parents. I was a young gay man in the suburbs, growing up in the middle of the AIDS crisis, and there was this amazing-looking woman on stage in a rubber dress and evening gloves at the Savoy, who ambushed the whole event with a speech about how the *Evening Standard*'s editorial stance was wickedly homophobic and stigmatizing of people with HIV and AIDS at that time. It was all done with a huge smile and if you turn the sound off, it looks like any other gracious acceptance speech, but because you were in a rubber dress and pearls and because of what you were saying, it was deeply subversive. Jarman was a cult figure for young queer people of the era, and his diary record of that night, published as part of *Smiling in Slow Motion* (2000), is brilliant: "The audience were gasping, her intervention so impressive she was joined by Shirley MacLaine, who left the ridiculous Bubbles Rothermere's party in support when she found out Sandy's ticket was torn up in her face." Tell me about the part that dress played in that event, and how you felt.

SANDY: Well, the *Evening Standard* always told people if they had won in advance, so I knew I was getting the award and would be on stage, and I had an opportunity to do something. I needed an outfit. I was friends with the latex designer Kim West and asked her to make me something glamorous. She came up with a full-length capped-sleeve dress that I wore with pearls and evening gloves and big hair. Doing evening dress in rubber was a way to subvert things. The dress was part of what I was going to do. It was about being naughty. It made me feel good, and I absolutely needed to feel dressed-up. It was the most terrifying thing I've ever had to do, but I had to do it. I wasn't thinking about any impact that might have on my career. I wasn't establishment. I was arthouse and independent. I was there for Derek and did it for him. He launched my career. I am sure some people decided not to employ me because of that evening, but equally there were people who had respect for it.

MARK: What happened to the dress?

SANDY: I carried on wearing it out for another two years. Then I was in New Orleans working on *Interview with the Vampire* (1994), wore it to a huge Halloween party, and it just sort of exploded on the dancefloor.

MARK: *Interview with the Vampire* is one of several films you did with Neil Jordan, and your first major Hollywood moment. One of the reasons you got the *Evening Standard* award was for your work with Neil on his earlier film *The Miracle* (1991), and then you did *The Crying Game* with him in 1992—both much lower budget than the Anne Rice adaptation.

Suit designed by Sandy Powell and
made by Ian Frazer Wallace, 2016.

We photographed the sequin dress and studded leather jacket that Jaye Davidson wears in *The Crying Game* [page 105]. You told me you found the sequin dress in a store in Covent Garden, and the jacket was something you owned and customized for yourself, but it became part of the transgender character of Dil. How often does your personal wardrobe end up on screen?

SANDY: Quite often, if it's a period piece—and by period, I mean the 1990s. The Thierry Mugler catsuit you photographed has been on screen several times [page 98]. It was last on an actor in *The Wolf of Wall Street* (2013) who was playing a prostitute, straddling Leonardo DiCaprio. Seeing my own clothes on screen is like a private joke. I like that something that has a history with me is having another life on screen. There's an antique ring that I bought at Grays in Mayfair years ago that has been worn by Natalie Portman playing Anne Boleyn, Judi Dench as Mrs Henderson, and Emily Blunt as Queen Victoria.

MARK: All those films would have had substantial budgets, and that's always in evidence in those lavish Tudor or nineteenth-century dresses, but the early work would have been done for next to nothing. Derek Jarman's films are now lauded as masterpieces and immensely influential, but *Caravaggio*, which was one of the most talked about films of the year when it came out in 1986, had a budget of under £450,000. At the time, Duran Duran were spending twice that on a three-minute pop video. All of you involved made it look ravishing.

There's the great story about Christopher Hobbs, the art director, painting a floor black and flooding the space to make it look like Vatican marble. Obviously, the lighting played a great part in how everything worked so well, but how did you manage to pull together a wardrobe that looked as lush as Caravaggio's actual paintings?

SANDY: We recreated a couple of the paintings as tableaux, and I dyed the fabrics to match the colors in the paintings, but other than that I think it was all down to the wonderful chiaroscuro lighting by the cinematographer, Gabriel Beristáin. I honestly didn't know what I was doing but was obviously inspired by and responded to Derek's vision. His reference for most of the film was Italian neorealist cinema—I remember him screening the 1948 *Bicycle Thieves* for us.

MARK: There's a generation now obsessed with Derek Jarman who weren't born when he was alive. There are also a lot of Home Counties types who now have an appreciation for his name and legacy but wouldn't have been comfortable at all with his political rage in the 1980s about Section 28, the homophobia of the government and media, and the way the AIDS crisis was being dealt with. People like you, Tilda Swinton, and Simon Costin, who all began as part of Jarman's inner circle, have all gone on to be major successes and part of the establishment. Take me back to the beginning of your story with Derek.

SANDY: I had been working with Lindsay Kemp, who I knew about from my obsession with David Bowie and their early work together. I saw Lindsey perform *Flowers* at the Roundhouse in the mid-1970s, and I knew I wanted to be part of that world. While I was at art school, he was teaching classes at the Pineapple Dance Studios in Covent Garden, and I signed up. Then I asked him if I could show him some of my work, we became friends, and I dropped out of Central Saint Martins. I worked on the costumes for Lindsay's shows on tour, dyeing things in hotel bathrooms and weathering them with a blow torch.

Then I went to work in London with a small theater company. I created the costumes for a punk-meets-eighteenth-century show at the ICA called *Rococo*, in 1983, and I invited Derek to come and see it. I had seen *Jubilee* (1978) and *The Tempest* (1979) and was aware that Lindsay and members of his company had been featured in both of them, as well as in *Sebastiane* (1976). I loved both the visual splendor and sense of anarchy in his films, and they were more theatrical than the mainstream, so for me it felt like a natural progression. Derek also seemed like he'd be an interesting person to work with. So I got his phone number via a mutual friend who had met him at Heaven, called him up, and invited him to the ICA. He came, then asked me to tea at his flat at Phoenix House, which is what he did with anyone he liked or was interested in. I said I wanted to do costumes for film, and he suggested I start by doing music videos.

The first thing I did with him was "Touch the Radio" for the band Language (1983), using all the costumes I made for *Rococo*. Then I worked with him on stuff for Wang Chung, Pet Shop Boys, and The Smiths. We did Bryan Ferry's "Windswept" in 1985, with a cast of dancers dressed as whirling dervishes, and I remember being so nervous because Ferry was so devastatingly good-looking. Then Derek started talking about making *Caravaggio*, and it just happened. Suddenly we were making a film.

MARK: Derek was obviously bringing his unique, queer perspective to the Caravaggio story. What were you bringing?

SANDY: It was instinctive. I was just working in the same way I had worked in theater when the Arts Council funded everything, which meant we had the resources to be experimental. Everything was unconventional but timeless. I had never worked on a conventional play, and there wasn't a strict way of researching period details—I was just creating costumes for whatever felt right for each person in each scene. Derek had a wonderful ability to communicate his ideas and vision, yet allow his collaborators the freedom to experiment, make mistakes, and make their own mark on the work.

MARK: What have you kept from the Jarman years?

SANDY: I have a *Caravaggio* costume that Nigel Terry wore, which was part of *PROTEST!*, the Derek Jarman retrospective in Dublin in 2019–20. I used to have the dress that Tilda wore in that film, but I lost it. I may have worn it to Kinky Gerlinky or something. That's often what happened. Things would be worn to parties and vanish. I have all of Tilda's costumes from *Edward II* (1991) and from *Wittgenstein* (1993). I'm glad I have those. It's a part of history.

MARK: What is the research process like when you're working with a substantial budget on what you once called at the Academy Awards "films about dead monarchs"? How do you go about sourcing textiles, and how has your process changed since you did *Orlando* in 1992 with Sally Potter?

SANDY: The research process has always been the same apart from the fact that we didn't have the internet in 1992. I still always begin with books. I have an extensive collection of books on costume, art, and photography. I find you can get inspiration for anything, regardless of the subject or period of the subject you are researching. I will begin by looking at the actual period either in paintings, or photographs if it is post mid-nineteenth century, then look further afield to contemporary fashion and modern art. Sometimes it's the combination of colors in a painting or in nature that will inspire a costume I don't have a silhouette for yet.

Finding the fabrics often starts way before I know what the costume is, and more often that will dictate the design. I love looking for fabrics myself, but often on bigger projects I employ buyers who have thousands of contacts and resources, and they bring me swatches to choose from. I do still always find the time to go to a fabric shop myself. It's one of my favorite things to do. That's when and where the ideas happen.

MARK: Often when you're working on a character, they are on a journey. How do you tell that part of the story through costume?

SANDY: Well, if you look at *Carol* (2015), Rooney Mara's character Therese Belivet has a trajectory. She starts out as young and slightly naïve, verging on Beatnik, but still conservative. Then she meets Carol, who is dead chic and confident, and becomes a little bit bolder, until she starts wearing tailored suits, like Cate Blanchett's character. But there are no rules to the way you develop a character, each one is different. It's much more interesting to work on a character that develops.

Sometimes that's just about how they wear something, and how it fits. When you talk about having a "fitting" with an actor, people assume that means getting everything to fit perfectly. But that's not what it is—it's about getting to grips with the character and what works for them. Maybe it's messy. Maybe they don't tuck their shirt in. Maybe their trousers are too short, too long, or too tight. Sometimes it's a certain style of jeans. When I was dressing Julianne Moore's character for *The Glorias* in 2020, I needed a certain bootcut of Levi's that were popular in the 1990s, but I couldn't find precisely what I wanted. Sometimes I ask myself why I'm agonizing over something that might be a minuscule detail, when an audience might not spot that an alternative was used. But while I'm working to please an audience, I'm working to please myself more. If I wasn't doing that, I couldn't do my job.

MARK: The costuming in *The Irishman* is nuanced but inherently restrained. But in something like *Orlando*, it is one of the most significant visual elements on screen. Likewise *The Favourite*, where it's a period piece, but deliberately monochrome, which brings a whole mood. Then there's *Far from Heaven* (2002), where every aspect of the color is so studied and lush.

SANDY: We had extensive meetings on that film about the production design and cinematography, studying the Douglas Sirk films that were the inspiration. Todd Haynes had a Pantone strip of color attached to each scene in the script. It wasn't necessarily a specific reference to something, like the wallpaper or a dress—it was just what was in his head and what he was feeling. So that was all we needed, to see those colors. I worked closely with the art department, and that goes for every film.

MARK: I'm interested in the relationship between fashion and film. The first time we ever spoke was after *Interview with the Vampire*, when we talked about Brad Pitt's fur-trimmed coat, how beautiful it was, and how lots of your male friends had said the same thing as me and wanted to own it. I have a theory that cinema sits above fashion in the hierarchy of influence. Designers constantly take from film—McQueen did a whole Givenchy collection in 1998 based on Sean Young's character in *Blade Runner*, and his menswear collection in 2009, *The McQueensbury Rules*, was based on one of your films, *Gangs of New York* (2002).

SANDY: Really? I had no idea about that! But I don't agree with the theory. I think film takes from fashion and fashion from film. It's not a hierarchy. I always look at fashion, for whatever period I'm doing. I use fashion photography as a reference. I need to be able to work out every aspect of something.

Meanwhile, my personal relationship with fashion has changed. I have young people who work with me who come in wearing a totally different outfit every day, while I like a uniform. I can't think about what I'm going to wear every day. I had a denim suit made by someone in New York, based on some of my favorite Comme des Garçons pieces, and I wear that all the time when I'm working. Derek was similar—he would always wear a boiler suit or a workwear jacket when he was filming. I don't like the idea of trends. I like Gaultier because he did the same things time and time again through his career, and never became old or boring. My go-to is always Comme des Garçons. I still wear the pieces I first bought in 1985, and they haven't dated because they're above fashion [**page 100**]. I don't like fashion for the sake of fashion. But ultimately the history of it is my passion and I am in the privileged position of getting paid to indulge in it.

The Signature Suit toile
designed by Sandy Powell,
made by Ian Frazer Wallace,
2016; signed 2020.

Elizabethan men's costume worn by Tilda Swinton in *Orlando* (1992).

Catsuit by Thierry
Mugler, *c.* 1990;
custom-made boots by
The Little Shoe Box,
London, *c.* 1991.

Shooting costume worn by
Rachel Weisz as Lady Sarah
in *The Favourite* (2017).

Jacket and skirt by Comme
des Garçons, *c.* 1985.

Green jersey dress by
Annie Hadley, 2004, a
replica of the mustard
yellow worn by
Cate Blanchett in
The Aviator (2004).

Breeches and bomber jacket by
Jean Paul Gaultier, *c.* 1989.

Jacket and shorts by
Val Piriou, *c.* 1990.

103

Corset jacket by Jean Paul
Gaultier, *c.* 1990; shorts by
Val Piriou, *c.* 1990.

Costume worn by Jaye Davidson in *The Crying Game* (1992). Sequined dress sourced from a Covent Garden vintage store; vintage leather jacket customized by Sandy Powell.

5 | Stephen Jones

It's a bold statement but difficult to disprove: Stephen Jones isn't just the most famous living hatmaker, he is without parallel in millinery history. Even Rose Bertin, who brought the art to the public's attention as Marie Antoinette's "Minister of Fashion" in the eighteenth century and made millinery a commercial entity, can't compare to what Jones has achieved in a career that spans over five decades. As well as putting his name to a spectacular body of work, he is considered by all who work with him to be a rare, true gentleman within the fashion industry.

Stephen Jones studied Women's Fashion at Saint Martin's School of Art in 1976 and opened his first Covent Garden boutique on Endell Street in 1980, close to the Blitz club with which he was synonymous alongside the likes of John Galliano, Boy George, Stephen Linard, John Maybury, and Steve Strange. Stephen Jones Millinery has maintained a presence in the area ever since. As well as his own seasonal ready-to-wear designs and couture, he has created hats for Comme des Garçons, Jean Paul Gaultier, Marc Jacobs, Thierry Mugler, and Schiaparelli, as well as private clients including Diana, Princess of Wales, Rihanna, Mick Jagger, and Lady Gaga. He has been milliner to the house of Dior since 1996, working with creative directors Maria Grazia Chiuri, John Galliano, Kim Jones, and Raf Simons. In 2009, he curated the V&A show *Hats: An Anthology by Stephen Jones*, which broke attendance records for the museum, and in 2010 MoMu in Antwerp launched a retrospective of his work, *Stephen Jones & The Accent of Fashion*. He has had solo exhibitions in Brighton, Brisbane, New York, Istanbul, and Salem, and in 2016 was the subject of the Rizzoli book *Stephen Jones: Souvenirs*. He was awarded an OBE in 2010.

Stephen Jones at The Beaumont Hotel, Mayfair, London.
Suit by Thom Browne; Coco beret by Stephen Jones Millinery, *Bonnes Vacances* collection, Spring/Summer 2022.

MARK: I'd like to hear about how you communicate with designers when you're working on pieces for them. When we first met in 1997, I brought Andrew Groves to see you after you kindly offered to create the hats for his first show, which I was producing, and the first thing you did was ask him to draw a bow, to gauge what his style was. Is that still a part of the process?

STEPHEN: No. Fashion isn't like that anymore. There isn't the same time for research and development. I rely on my intuition and experience. The whole conversation about a bow was about observing someone's character—did they prefer something geometric, or perhaps more baroque? Despite whatever romantic notion people have about designers, no one is Cristóbal Balenciaga spending six months sketching a sleeve anymore. They are all sniffing out the mood of the moment and then making a leap. There used to be the potential to play with fashion, but that's an expensive thing to do. The only way that fashion makes sense is if it reflects the time in which it takes place.

MARK: You have long-standing relationships with major houses but, as you did with Andrew Groves, you're still generous enough with your time and resources to work with young designers who aren't operating under the auspices of the big Paris corporations, like Matty Bovan and John Alexander Skelton. If they're not drawing a bow for you now, how do you establish a dialogue someone you haven't worked with before? The work you've created for those designers I just mentioned is brilliant but graphically couldn't be more different—I'm thinking about the net headpieces full of helium balloons for Matty for his Autumn/Winter 2018 show, which he said was about carrying the weight of the world, and the folded newspaper hat that you did for John for Spring/Summer 2022, which was a collection based on Ted Hughes and poems he wrote about West Yorkshire. One is theatrical and exuberant; the other is dour but witty.

STEPHEN: I'm not coming from a neutral place, and the designers aren't coming from one either. I'm sixty-five, so people have a perception of me—in a funny way, some designers want me to walk in and dictate, "Yes, the sky is blue," and then for both of us to have an expression of freedom through the work, but then they'll say: "Yeah, but I want a matador hat." So that's what we do.

I see John Skelton as a successor to Hussein Chalayan, in a way. He is all about research and goes on a path that is unique and magical. It is evident in his shows—from the handwriting on the invitations to the model casting, it's all precise. He is telling a story. Grace Wales Bonner is similar, where everything is studied: "What does the top stitch represent?" It is about symbols. Matty Bovan is about experimentation and doesn't like to guide me quite so much; he is quite playful. Every designer has their point of view, which is what makes working with them so interesting.

MARK: You have a unique position in the industry. There are great milliners working, like Philip Treacy and Prudence in London, and Albertus Swanepoel in New York, but no one else has been involved in so many collaborations and come up with pieces that are consistently unique, rather than just bringing their brand and style to someone else. One wonders if there'll be anyone around who can do what you do, when you aren't here anymore. Some designers, I'm sure, want Stephen Jones Millinery to be a part of their canon more than they actually want hats.

STEPHEN: Well, there's Noel Stewart and Philip, and their millinery is unique and extraordinary. For me, it's not about the hat, it's about how it transforms someone. People asked me how I could have worked with Comme des Garçons and John Galliano at the same time, but it's just like going to a party and having different conversations on the same evening.

MARK: Studying some of the pieces we have photographed from your archive, it's wild to see the detail on them. The Comme des Garçons piece is extraordinary, not just because of the raffia you used to make it, but because there is a joint Comme and Stephen Jones label inside, which is incredibly rare [**page 115**]. The first time I went to Tokyo, I found a jacket in a shop in Omotesandō that had a Comme and Vivienne Westwood collaborative label, and I've never been able to find details on how that came about. Rei Kawakubo was always so protective of her brand. How did you first connect with her?

STEPHEN: Well, the hat we shot is a remake of the 1984 original, from my first season working with her. When we relaunched them last year, I asked if we could have a joint label and she said yes, which was amazing.

I met Rei after my first trip to Tokyo, where I was doing an exhibition at the Isetan store. In those days I had a habit of getting immersed in conversations with people and staying too late at parties, and my assistant Sibylle de Saint Phalle used to tell me that I needed to learn how to say "Thank you" and walk away. Sibylle and I were flying back to London from Tokyo, and because you couldn't fly over Russian airspace at the time, the plane went via Alaska. We were in Duty Free in Anchorage airport when a woman came over to me and said she liked my hats, and I did as I was advised, saying "Thank you" and then walking away. And it happened twice. Then Sibylle ran over to me and said, "You idiot, that was Rei Kawakubo!" So we talked and agreed to stay in touch, then got back on the plane. I turned right into Economy with Sibylle, and Rei turned left into First class.

I began working with her shortly afterwards. It was before the invention of the fax machine, so any time I did a sketch it had to be couriered to Tokyo, and because it was a sketch it was invoiceable and took five days to get there. It was a laborious process. I can't remember the precise brief, but I knew we wanted to use natural materials.

MARK: The perception of Comme des Garçons has changed radically since it was that rarefied and exclusive entity in the 1980s. Adrian Joffe has made it into a global brand, with so much product at so many different price points, via Dover Street Market. What do you think about that shift?

STEPHEN: It is changing with the times. I remember Amanda Verdan, who was the buying director of Harvey Nichols in the 1980s, telling me that they would buy a lot of Mugler and Montana, but if a customer came in and tried on a dress and they didn't have the matching shoes in stock in the right size, the client wouldn't buy the outfit. For the customer, there was no point if you couldn't buy the complete look as shown on the runway. You were investing in the designer's vision, like becoming part of a painting. That vision of fashion now seems ridiculous, although wonderful in its way, too. People used to buy Comme des Garçons because it was Rei's great vision of how she wanted to change the world, and now they buy Comme because it's a Play Converse sneaker. Even if you are young and know nothing about fashion, you know it's a respectable fashion label. And it's a good logo.

MARK: We've photographed one hat to represent each of the designers you've worked with at Dior [pages 119–121 and page 123]. Let's talk about how different each one has been to work with.

STEPHEN: Maria Grazia Chiuri is amazing. She has overseen the most sizeable wholesale business of any hat collection of any major luxury house. She comes from an accessories background, so sees everything as a product—how it looks in store and relates to the client and the rest of the collection. Maria's idea for Dior prêt-à-porter was extraordinary: she wanted the hats to be for every girl in the world, and everything had to be easy to pack in a suitcase. You couldn't put any of John's work in a suitcase, it needed its own box. Now they have repeat orders of 5,000 of a single style. Hat designs almost never go into commercial production on that scale. It happened with Marc by Marc, but it's rare.

My relationship with Kim Jones is funny, because he grew up buying *The Face* and *i-D*, and he saw me in those magazines in the same way that I used to buy Roxy Music albums when I was his age, dreaming about being a part of another world. All of that is now part of our relationship, and it's an honor to work with him. Raf Simons' story at Dior was fascinating. When he came to the house, I was the only person he knew there—we had worked together at Jil Sander. He was coming in after John, who had done so many statement hats, and Raf wanted to create his own identity for Dior, as is right. He liked the mid-century gesture of millinery as an expression of couture elegance, but from a slightly postmodern perspective. When Gianfranco Ferré was at Dior it was all about women with their hair styled in a chignon, like grand polite ladies. When I was working with Raf, we made bonnets in black and white to go with the famous Miss Dior dress, covered in flowers.

MARK: John Galliano has been a part of your story since the 1980s. How different was he to know and work with when he was part of the empire of Dior, compared to being an independent entity in London in the 1980s?

STEPHEN: Well, John has always been a genius and the head of his empire. There's always been a sense of greatness, whether realized or not. He has always painted with a big brush.

MARK: The scarab beetle piece we photographed is from the Egyptian show he did in 2004, which was the apogee of Dior haute couture excess.

STEPHEN: That collection represented a change in fashion. Fashion used to follow a distinct path—clothing was shown, appeared in editorial, then went on sale and lived in your wardrobe. There is now an extra stage for some clothes, which is that they appear in a museum and are appreciated as sculpture or as works of art. All the clothes by John at Dior hold their own in a museum context. Each is like a fully formed movie.

Fashion has moved on from that now—but then you have someone like Matty Bovan who is showing extravagant pieces, so the spirit is still there. The brief from Monsieur Arnault to John was to make Dior the most famous fashion house in the world, which he did. The photograph of Erin O'Connor wearing a gold crown in that Egyptian show was on the cover of seventy-two newspapers around the world.

MARK: The crown you made for Vivienne Westwood for her *Harris Tweed* show in 1987 has been the subject of considerable controversy and become part of fashion history [**page 117**]. It's as much a part of her story as being arrested after the Sex Pistols boat party on the Queen's Silver Jubilee in 1977, or Naomi Campbell falling off her heels on the catwalk in 1993.

STEPHEN: I had known Vivienne since the days of the Seditionaries store. At first we were talking about millinery techniques and stiffening fabric. Then she mentioned that she was interested in creating the mini-crini skirt, which was based on a little petticoat that Luciana Martinez had shown her. We both liked Walt Disney, and I pointed out to her that all Disney illustrations are based on circles. It's like if you look at a baby's face—it's all circles. So that's where she started developing the idea for the polka dots for the *Mini-Crini* collection in 1985. It was also the starting point for the *Harris Tweed* crown.

As I recall, Philip Sallon had been wearing a crown constructed from white napkins, which had interested Vivienne. She said the inspiration for her next show was going to be the royal family, and she wanted me to create a crown. I worked on a pattern and the silhouette, but it involved so many pieces and so much time that it wasn't financially feasible to manufacture. Vivienne said she could have students do the cutting and stitching for pieces for the shop, and I made around ten or so for the show. I was then away in Paris working, and heard nothing.

Then ten years later there was Jane Mulvagh's biography *Vivienne Westwood: An Unfashionable Life* (1998), with the story of the hats arriving for the show and Vivienne having a complete fit when she saw my labels inside the crowns. She had them taken out and replaced with hers, and I wasn't in the show credits. Steven Philip gave me the crown we photographed, made from a pinstriped fabric. It's a rare piece. He also had the pattern that was used, which still had my writing on it.

After all that, when it came to the V&A retrospective of Vivienne's work in 2004, she didn't want me credited for the famous Nick Knight photograph of Sara Stockbridge in the crown, which was on the cover of *i-D* in 1987.

I'm by no means the most original designer in the world, and everyone copies, but I always remember the line from Boris Lermontov in *The Red Shoes*: "It is worth remembering, that it is much more disheartening to have to steal than to be stolen from."

MARK: That particular crown now has an added poignancy attached to it as a single object as well as a design, because it's what you wore to Vivienne's memorial service at Southwark Cathedral. It would have been the first time many people had seen it. It was a statement for you to wear it, along with a pair of bondage trousers, because it links you so strongly to her history and legacy. As indeed it should. You were integral to it. But there is a strange and intense issue around ownership and authorship attached to everything that came out of 430 Kings Road in all its iterations, from the Let it Rock store that Westwood opened with Malcolm McLaren in 1971 to Worlds End today. When that V&A show opened, McLaren's name was absent from all the exhibition credits on show, even though all the labels in the clothes up until 1984 had both their surnames on it.

In 2021, I spent a couple of months researching a story for the *New York Times* on the industry of forgeries being sold as 1970s designs attributed to the pair. The whole business is Machiavellian, but also a little sad. There was an anonymous email sent to McLaren in 2008 from "Minnie Minx," apparently exposing parties involved in the business of making fake punk clothes, including a once promising Saint Martins graduate, as well as a member of McLaren's own family. There was then a high-profile case in which McLaren told Damien Hirst that everything Hirst had bought from one of the people mentioned was fake. Initially the motives seemed financial, partly because of a lucrative market in Japan for stuff that wasn't readily available in terms of original, authentic product, and because there were a lot of people who wanted to buy it. But there also seemed to be a desire by some of the protagonists to attach themselves to something that felt important to them. It was an aspiration that worked both ways—the forgers had been obsessive about the designs and by recreating them they were in some way becoming a part of what they loved, while the gullible buyers just wanted to believe they owned something resonant. McLaren's widow Young Kim said something significant: "All these men—and it's always men—want to own punk." And it's funny that one of the ways to identify the fakes is by their size. McLaren and Westwood made their clothes to fit their own diminutive frames, and the fakes are sized up for portly ex-punks.

STEPHEN: Well, punk is still seen as the ultimate period of rebellion, particularly for some middle-aged people who wish they were still one of the wild young things. But the history of punk remains interesting. Everyone has their own version. It was a gay movement as much as anything. Punk was about people desperate to reinvent themselves. It was young and raw. Really, I think Philip Sallon invented punk. Richard Torry, the knitwear designer and musician, was also a big part of it. He produced a lot of work for Vivienne. But nothing would have happened without her. There wouldn't have been a Galliano without a Westwood, and without Galliano there wouldn't have been a McQueen. That's the legacy. She was brilliant.

MARK: There's a whimsical nature to the crown that runs through a lot of your work. That sense of English eccentricity has massive appeal. Tell me about the diorama of the garden that features in the Gazebo hat from 1994 that we photographed [**page 124**].

STEPHEN: It is novelty and indulgence. It comes from growing up in the late 1960s and 1970 and watching black-and-white films and musicals on BBC2. It's about a kind of cute formality.

MARK: Another of the pieces we photographed is Seams Like a Dream, named after the 1980 Swanky Modes fashion show you were a part of, at Notre Dame Hall off Leicester Square [**page 118**]. Swanky Modes was run by four women—Judy Dewsbury, Melanie Herberfield, Willie Walters, and Esme Young—and isn't given enough credit in fashion history. In 1978, they designed white silk garments with black tyre prints running at angles across them. I showed some pictures to Simon Ungless, who did all the early prints for McQueen, because they were almost identical to the work he did for *The Birds* collection for Lee in Spring/ Summer 1995. Simon had never seen the Swanky Modes pieces before and was amazed. They were ahead of their time. His concept had come from the scene in the Hitchcock film where the birds attack and cars are crashing everywhere as people try to escape. The graphics inhabit different worlds, decades apart, but I think the parallels show how good Swanky Modes was.

STEPHEN: I always thought Seams Like a Dream was a fantastic title. Swanky Modes represented the generation before me. I came from the middle of nowhere, and then suddenly I met Derek Jarman, Andrew Logan, and Brian Eno through that scene. It was a generation that taught us how to party, how to blag your way into a club and get a free drink, all of which is important when you're growing up. I saw the Swanky Modes aesthetic as being like a Duggie Fields painting come to life. They took PVC and 1950s sex magazines and made fashion from it. Vivienne Westwood was doing something similar with SEX on the Kings Road, but she was serious, and Swanky Modes was playful.

MARK: Your archive is a whole history of London fashion, documenting how the business as well as style has changed.

STEPHEN: The hat you photographed, Tit-tat/82, is a remake of the second hat I ever had on the cover of a magazine [**page 116**]. The first was a beret that Mario Testino shot for *Ms London*, which was his first ever published work. Tit-tat/82 was styled by Michael Roberts for the December 1982 issue of *Tatler* and shot by Terence Donovan. I had been getting press in *The Face* and *i-D*, but not the more established magazines. When you went to *Vogue* or *Harpers & Queen* as a designer, they asked you how many stockists you had, and if you didn't have at least five in the UK, you couldn't appear in the magazine. It was totally different from now, where everyone wants the most exclusive thing.

Michael Roberts had an arrangement at the time with Robert Forrest at Browns so that anything he photographed for *Tatler* would be bought by the shop on South Molton Street. So they bought the hat. That's how we circumnavigated the rules. They were my dream team and the people who made it happen.

MARK: One thing we haven't discussed is how you dress. From pictures of you at the Blitz and when you had your first store in the basement of PX, through to any time I've seen you in person, everything looks so considered and perfect. I can't imagine you in jeans and a T-shirt. Do you dress to help you feel a certain way to create the work?

STEPHEN: I do wear jeans and T-shirts. I can wear Japanese denim and a Prada jacket with a hat, and the hat gives it power. I always think about how to dress for the situation I am going to be in and how I need to communicate with people. I've been working with Thom Browne for years, and I wear his suits because they make me feel very dressed-up when I'm not mentally feeling dressed-up [**page 106**]. They give me a feeling of structure. And that's the power of tailoring. If I was wearing pajamas I wouldn't feel on duty. Clothes, like hats, help you feel the way you want to feel.

Stephen Jones Millinery
for Comme des Garçons,
Spring/Summer 1984.

115

Tit-tat/82 by Stephen Jones Millinery, *Time Travel* collection, Autumn/Winter 2006.

116

Stephen Jones Millinery for
Vivienne Westwood, *Harris Tweed*
collection, Autumn/Winter 1987.

117

Seams Like a Dream by Stephen
Jones Millinery, *E=MC2* collection,
Spring/Summer 1998.

118

Stephen Jones Millinery for Dior
Haute Couture (John Galliano),
Spring/Summer 2004.

Stephen Jones Millinery
for Dior Haute Couture
(Raf Simons),
Spring/Summer 2013.

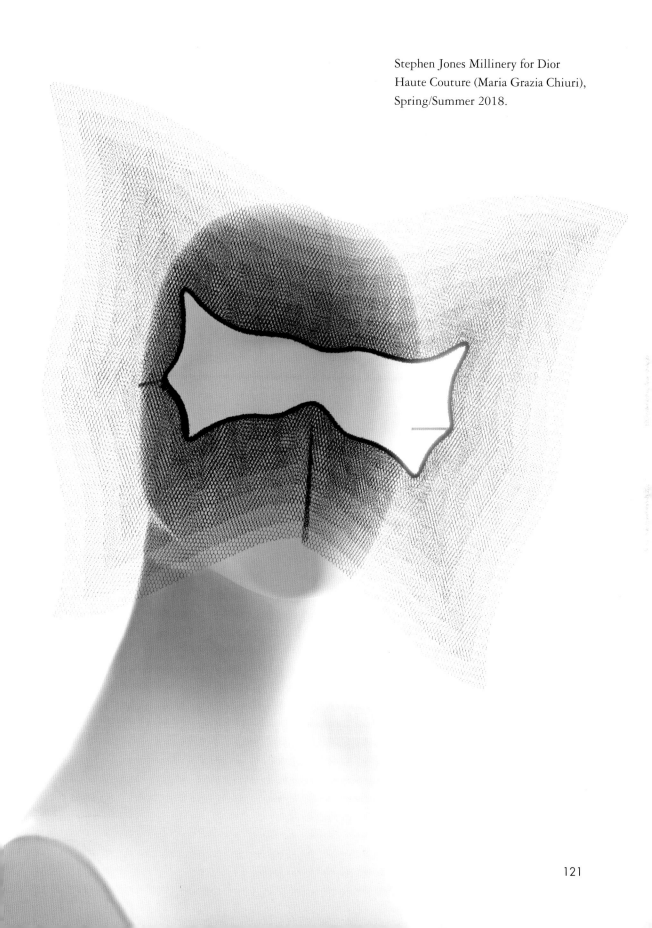

Stephen Jones Millinery for Dior
Haute Couture (Maria Grazia Chiuri),
Spring/Summer 2018.

Angel or Devil 2 by
Stephen Jones Millinery,
It's About Time! collection,
Autumn/Winter 2020.

122

Stephen Jones
Millinery for Dior
Men (Kim Jones),
Spring/Summer 2020.

Gazebo by Stephen Jones
Millinery, *Rococo Futura*
collection,
Autumn/Winter 1994.

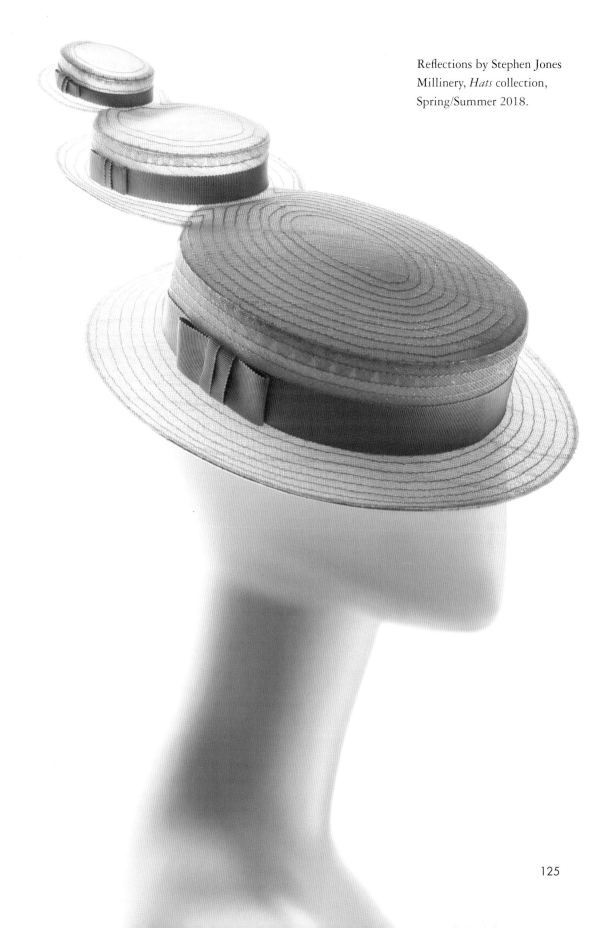

6 | Carla Sozzani

The term "muse" is used frequently in fashion but is often amorphous or a pretension. Sometimes it refers to a model favored by a certain designer; often it's a fancified noun for a stylist.

Carla Sozzani has been a true muse. She was a constant source of inspiration for the late Azzedine Alaïa, as well as a close friend, and omnipresent throughout his career in Paris. More than that, she is a visionary who changed the way fashion is presented and retailed. She opened 10 Corso Como in 1990, initially as a gallery in a part of central Milan then considered unfashionable. It expanded into a concept store, followed by a café, restaurant, and hotel. The retail element developed to carry avant-garde and exclusive designs at a variety of price points long before others followed the format.

Prior to opening 10 Corso Como, Sozzani was the editor-in-chief of all special issues of *Vogue Italia* and involved with the launch of Romeo Gigli's label in the mid-1980s. She was appointed American *Vogue*'s editor-at-large for Italy by Alexander Liberman and then became founding editor-in-chief of Italian *Elle* in 1987. Carla's sister Franca Sozzani was the feted editor-in-chief of *Vogue Italia* and passed away in 2016.

In 2016, Carla launched Fondazione Sozzani, an institute housing her remarkable collection of art, fashion, and photography. Her personal fashion archive now numbers over 5,000 pieces. She worked with Azzedine Alaïa from 1998 until his death in 2017, helping to curate exhibitions of his work in Florence in 1996 and at the Azzedine Alaïa Foundation in Paris, where she remains President. Carla Sozzani continues to be based in Milan.

Carla Sozzani at home in Milan.

Coat by Azzedine Alaïa from his last collection, Spring/Summer 2018.

MARK: Since Azzedine passed, you've been involved in curating shows about his work, including one focused on what he was doing before he became famous in Paris in the 1980s. Tell me about that curation work.

CARLA: Azzedine never saw himself as a teacher, but the more I thought about how important he was in fashion, the clearer it became to me that his whole life served as a lesson for young designers. He had such a vision of what he wanted to do from the very beginning. Before being famous, and far from any notion of being rich, he just wanted to be an exceptional couturier. The ephemera from his work in the era before the 1980s is fascinating.

MARK: He shared numerous interests with his friend, the furniture designer Pierre Paulin. They were both fascinated by ergonomics, and Azzedine was a pioneer of stretch fabrics. He defined the body-conscious 1980s with highly sexualized leather pieces for women, but unlike Versace and Mugler—as great as they were—there was never a hint of the meretricious or the misogynist about his work, and in fact Alaïa was always revered for being better than the industry in which he is deified. What do you think the changes were in his aesthetic from that period through to his final years?

CARLA: Like all intelligent people, he knew perfection was not possible, so he was never satisfied, but he did become more and more refined during his career. There are two periods of Alaïa—the 1980s and early 1990s work, and then when he started again after 2000, when he became more obsessive about the construction, when he was striving for a new kind of restrained perfection. He could work on a jacket for months and throw it away because he wasn't happy with it.

MARK: I remember an academic friend telling me about taking a group of students from London to see the first show you curated at the Alaïa space after Azzedine passed away, and he had a long conversation with them about the clothes being free from ego. They were engineered entirely to make a woman feel beautiful and powerful. That's not been a priority for many designers. Often, they just want to make a statement.

CARLA: He wanted to offer security to women, and always did it with respect. If you feel secure, that makes you feel beautiful and happy. He always used to tell me, "It's important to feel comfortable."

Carla Sozzani at home in Milan.
Coat by Azzedine Alaïa from his last collection, Spring/Summer 2018.

MARK: What was your initial communication with him? How did you become a team?

CARLA: It was when I was director of special editions of *Vogue Italia*. Somebody from *Elle* told me I should absolutely do a story on this new designer that was working with leather and studs. The first story I did on him was November 1981. In 1987, I was fired from Italian *Elle* for putting a long black dress by him on a cover we shot with Paolo Roversi. It was a problem for them because he was seen as a "foreign" designer, and one without an advertising budget. In tribute he called that dress the Carla.

MARK: How would you describe your main role at the studio?

CARLA: I was the girl with the pompoms, standing beside him and shouting: "Azzedine, you're the best!" As you know, visionaries need teams, and in 1999, to make sure that Azzedine could continue, I contacted Lineapiù, the Italian yarn company who used to work with him on developing new concepts, and they then helped him financially. But I realized he needed stronger support, so I spoke to Prada, and in 2000 they bought Azzedine's company, which allowed him to buy back his building in the Marais where the Foundation is today. It gave him freedom in his work, and the relationship with them allowed us to develop the Alaïa shoes business.

When Prada and Azzedine decided to take separate paths in 2007, I contacted Richemont, who bought the company and eventually the brand in 2010. Over these years I was always next to Azzedine to oversee the *intemporels* [perennial core] collections and shoes, bags, and accessories, so Azzedine would be free to dedicate himself to couture. The work he created in that later period was astoundingly beautiful, even more perfect than before.

MARK: Did you start wearing his clothes as soon as you met?

CARLA: Yes. At the time I was at *Vogue Italia*, and I still have the first couture dress he made for me. It is wool jersey with buttons at the back. I remember the fitting—he measured my chest, then moved to my waist and laughed: "Wow! Huge! *Very* Mediterranean!" But I never liked to be too body-conscious. I mixed Comme des Garçons with Alaïa, so my look was both tight and voluminous.

MARK: There was a whole period in fashion when models had to look emaciated to be successful. Now we embrace different body shapes. How do you feel about that? There are constant cultural shifts with this. In Elizabethan times they padded clothing to make you look fatter, and therefore richer.

CARLA: I think we are, fortunately, in a time of freedom. What is important is not what you weigh, it's what you feel. It's better to be a little fatter and have a nice smile. When it comes to health, you should absolutely exercise. But if it's just aesthetics, it doesn't make any sense to me to deny yourself happiness.

MARK: The fit of couture is unique—as is so much about it. How different is it for you to wear Alaïa couture compared to something off the peg?

CARLA: First of all, there's the fact that it is one of a kind, which makes it inherently desirable—it is made just for you, to fit you, so you feel spoilt. Then there's the perfection of Azzedine's cut. I cannot say enough about this, because many young designers working on computers do not have any relationship to the fabric or the way scissors cut through it and shape a piece. It was always a pleasure to watch Azzedine work—fitting, cutting, refitting, pinning. When you look inside, it's not like any other dress. The construction inside is remarkable. It could take him 120 hours to make one special item.

MARK: Do you have much couture by other designers?

CARLA: I have other designers of course, starting from the first Yves Saint Laurent collections, through to Walter Albini, but apart from Alaïa, I primarily admire designers who have worked in ready to wear: Comme des Garçons, Martin Margiela, Yohji Yamamoto, Junya Watanabe, Vivienne Westwood. The philosophy of their design is carried into everything they do. What draws me to really want a piece is my respect for the attitude and intelligence of the designer. Azzedine's respect and love for the women he designed for, and sense of design intuition in every element of his work, are compelling.

MARK: You've spent your career working in fashion in a variety of roles as a stylist, editor, designer, and retailer. All of it has been in the world of high fashion. What is your perspective on fast fashion?

CARLA: Sustainability is a major issue. But I can see change. The young want something that is of higher quality now, that they choose with love—they want clothes that have meaning and can last a long time. We live in a time when we just don't need that many clothes.

MARK: There's an irony there, because you have a warehouse with over 5,000 museum-quality gowns by the most important designers of the last 100 years.

CARLA: Even then, I haven't kept everything. I wore a lot of Pucci in the 1960s, and also clothes from Rina Modelli, an atelier in Milan that made things from couture patterns from Paris. I gave those away and that's no loss. I don't want to use the word "collecting" because that's a big statement, but I first started keeping clothes when I discovered Saint Laurent in 1967. I felt a sense that those clothes were timeless, and I couldn't part with them. It was the same with Kenzo, and then of course Azzedine, Comme des Garçons, Vivienne Westwood, and Yohji Yamamoto. I also bought pieces that I never wore, but that I fantasized about wearing. I have so many Manolo Blahnik shoes, all unworn, because I don't like to wear heels, but they are beautiful objects.

MARK: When did you first develop an emotional connection to clothes?

CARLA: When I started wearing Comme des Garçons and Yohji Yamamoto in 1981. I had some pieces from Montana around the same time, which were beautiful, but they never gave me the same sense of confidence. Comme and Yohji were a revelation because I never liked makeup and I never liked heels, and neither were a part of the Japanese aesthetic.

MARK: Do you see the death of Azzedine as the end of a chapter for the house? It has carried on in a new form, with Peter Mulier as the first Creative Director in Azzedine's absence.

CARLA: Azzedine would have closed the Maison, for sure, if he had survived but not been able to work. But personally, I think there is so much in the archives, and so many people working there, it is good to keep it going. I also don't feel as sad as I might because he left us at the height of his powers. But then, we will never know, because he was always so innovative. A fashion designer usually makes drawings, but Azzedine never did that. He was an artist who just happened to work on the body, as a sculptor.

MARK: While you were friends with Azzedine, you were also working with Romeo Gigli, one of the most revered designers of his generation, who mixed the influence of different continents in a lush way, before Rifat Ozbek and Haider Ackermann. When his business failed, 10 Corso Como was founded in what was previously Spazio Romeo Gigli. The whole history of the intricacies of your relationship would fill a sizeable book, but I'm interested most in hearing how you'd describe Gigli's aesthetic to people who aren't familiar with it today.

CARLA: It was all about color and shape, and the image we both had of a Renaissance woman. The vision was informed by integrity and purity. We worked closely together for an intense period, and then it vanished and disappeared. But that was forty years ago. I like to look forward.

MARK: It is interesting how lives in fashion develop. A lot of people think Gigli has become a recluse and must be bitter about all the various licenses that have changed hands, putting his name on things that have nothing to do with him. But I met him recently in Marrakech, where he moved a few years ago from Milan, and he is happy and focused on furniture design. He says his past was so rooted in finding fabrics on his travels that he couldn't find now. But he makes clothing for himself, with fabrics he finds in Morocco. And he is still all about creating design and imagery, but in a different way.

And so many things are done in a different way now. Much of your own career has been spent working in the creation of fashion imagery, with amazing photographers. Images once had to give currency to a magazine for a month, now they pass much faster. The life, and lifespan, of imagery in fashion has changed more profoundly than the people behind its creation. Do images still have the same power when they are consumed at that rate?

CARLA: An image on Instagram is gone in a second. If I was going back to editorial today, I would work mostly with illustrators. Illustration gives you the possibility to dream more, it takes your mind in different directions. It takes time to do and has a different energy. I remember watching Grace Coddington at all the shows, drawing constantly in her little book, and being fascinated.

MARK: 10 Corso Como was pioneering and has a very social aspect to it. It's not just about racks of clothes, although its strength has also been about the potential to discover the work of a designer you aren't familiar with. What's going to happen in the future, in terms of bricks-and-mortar retail in fashion?

CARLA: There are two ways of shopping. Online is fast and easy, it comes to your house, and you can return it. But then you are only using one of your five senses with that experience. I don't like loud music in a shop, but I like 10 Corso Como because you can talk with people, and you shouldn't be rushing to buy another T-shirt, you should go and appreciate the moment. In the future, we will still need to be able to enjoy all the senses—to touch fabric, to smell a fragrance, to taste a wine.

MARK: It's interesting that there are several designers who think along the same lines as you, and who won't allow their work to be sold online—they insist you see it and touch it in person, even though they could make more money by allowing e-commerce. But those are just a handful of niche labels. The fashion industry as a whole is fairly cynical and has a short-term focus on profits. Are you optimistic about the future of fashion?

CARLA: Absolutely. Otherwise, I would stop! My daughter Sara is working a lot with new talent. I think that many people have something to say, but the system has made it difficult to be an entrepreneur while also keeping your integrity. When Rei Kawakubo and Yves Saint Laurent began, the world was much smaller. You sold your clothes to Italy, France, Germany, and New York. Today it's much bigger. Lots of talented people go to work for big houses to feel protected, but that kills the singular voice because they have to embrace the point of view of that house. But there will always be new talent, and it will always find a way.

Felt dress with vertical
laser cuts by Maison
Martin Margiela,
Autumn/Winter 1990.

White stretch top with shaped velvet
flowers by Comme des Garçons,
Abstract Excellence collection, Spring/
Summer 2004; white lace cage skirt by
Comme des Garçons, *White Drama*
collection, Spring/Summer 2012.

Felt coat by Comme des
Garçons, *Dimensions* collection,
Autumn/Winter 2012.

Beaded bias-cut silk dress
by Yohji Yamamoto,
*Hommage to Parisian
Couture and its
Icons* collection,
Spring/Summer 1997.

Gold embroidered shawl and
embroidered velvet couture
coat by Romeo Gigli,
Autumn/Winter 1989.

Dress by Maison
Martin Margiela,
Autumn/Winter 2006.

Gold embroidered shawl and
velvet intertwined ribbons
cocoon coat by Romeo Gigli,
Autumn/Winter 1989.

One of a kind top and skirt made from vintage silk scarves by Maison Martin Margiela (Artisanal), Spring/Summer 1992.

Dress by Azzedine Alaïa
Couture, 2011.

142

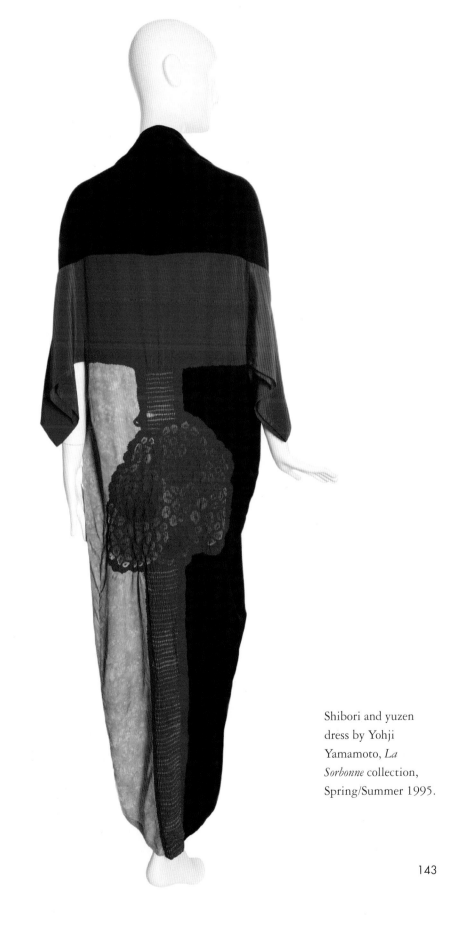

Shibori and yuzen
dress by Yohji
Yamamoto, *La
Sorbonne* collection,
Spring/Summer 1995.

Toga dress by Worlds End
(Malcolm McLaren and
Vivienne Westwood), *Buffalo/
Nostalgia of Mud* collection,
Autumn/Winter 1982.

Python dress by Azzedine
Alaïa Couture, 2008.

7 | Winn Austin

From 1989 to 1994, London nightlife was defined by a single nightclub: Kinky Gerlinky. The party was sporadic, growing from a one-off and effectively private gathering at a small space in Mayfair to a ballroom-scale event at the Empire in Leicester Square. It was launched by Michael and Gerlinde Costiff, counterculture figures in London since the early 1970s. After Gerlinde passed away in 1994, Michael went on to open World Archive concessions at international branches of Dover Street Market. The individual most linked to Kinky Gerlinky, aside from the Costiffs, is Winn Austin, who was host and MC for each event. A transgender model from Guyana, Winn has worked with numerous fashion designers including Pam Hogg and Rifat Ozbek. She acted in Todd Haynes's *Velvet Goldmine* (1998), featured in Claire Lawrie's 2018 documentary *Beyond "There's always a black issue Dear"*, has styled numerous Bollywood film productions, and volunteers for the Stonewall housing charity in London. In 2021, she launched Ms A with designer Bok Goodall, a lingerie and swimwear line for transgender women.

Winn Austin at Bob Bob Ricard, London.
Bodysuit by Ms A; vintage tailcoat and boots by Vivienne Westwood.

MARK: The first time I saw you was at London Fashion Week in 1992, modeling for Pam Hogg. It was the first fashion show I had ever been to and it felt like the most glamorous, exciting moment ever, with club kids on the runway next to professional models.

You've been around for so many different eras of fashion in London and seen a radical shift in gender politics. When Pam had that show, we were still using the term "drag" for transgender women—which now seems archaic and derogatory. Did you see it as that?

WINN: No. I've never felt like I needed to be validated by anyone. I've also always been a positive person and focused on ways to get past obstacles. I've been in rooms where a person of color or a transgender person would not usually be welcome, but I get past those things.

MARK: Clothes are obviously a big part of that positivity. Looking around your flat on Warren Street, it's obvious that these things mean a lot to you, and that you hold on to things.

WINN: I've always been a magpie, archivist, and hoarder. My wardrobe represents my past and present. I have a lot of gowns by Jeffrey Bryant, because he's great at cutting for my shape [pages 156, 163 and 165]. I have a cerise sequin suit Rifat Ozbek gave me, which I wore to the opening of the Versace store in London in 1995—Alicia Silverstone had worn it to an event before me, but he said I should keep it because I looked so amazing in it [page 158]. Rifat took me to the British Fashion Awards in his Turkish coin dress in 1992, when he won British Designer of the Year. He was always so clever in the way he took inspiration from people like Leigh Bowery and the club scene, but he was also influenced by his Turkish heritage. He was way ahead of his time.

I also have several pieces by Pam Hogg [page 162]. I wore the slashed bridal gown for the finale of the 1992 show, before she retired for a while. I also modeled for her at Freemasons' Hall in 2018.

MARK: There's a lot of stuff that is quite DIY. You've never been about just wearing a dress by a designer.

WINN: I make everything my own, whether by adding to it or accessorizing. Sometimes it's created just for me. I have a red velvet gown I wore to the premiere of *Too Wong Foo* in 1995 that I had made from the curtains in Porchester Hall, where I won my first drag pageant in the mid-1980s. I went to a party one night in the early 1990s and found out that they were closing and gutting the interior, so I said I wanted the drapes. My friend Tim Perkins, who used to work for Vivienne Westwood and who is now a costume cutter for the *Mission: Impossible* and *Indiana Jones* films, worked with me to create something unique [page 159].

MARK: What are the pieces in your wardrobe that you find most poignant?

WINN: There's a white fur wrap that you photographed which I had made when I was going to host Alexander McQueen's Christmas party in 2009, but it was canceled [page 164]. He died two months later. They gave me one of his skull-print chiffon scarves, which is now one of my most cherished possessions. I love how things come my way by fate, like the bias-cut dress we shot the white fur wrap with, which I saw in the window of a charity shop in Marlow in Buckinghamshire—it looks like a 1930s design, but it's actually a contemporary piece made, I suspect, for a wedding. The workmanship inside is extraordinary—couture-quality. It was £28, so I bought it immediately. I also have a gold fringed bustier that used to belong to Helena Springs who was a backing singer with Bob Dylan, the Pet Shop Boys, and Bette Midler. I used to rent her flat and she had left a whole bunch of costumes there. They represent happy memories.

MARK: I worked with you on projects when I was at film school, around about the time the tabloids were running stories comparing you to Naomi Campbell. It was all sensationalized along the lines of "You won't believe your eyes …." The credits on my films used your male birth name, which is also what we all called you at the time, and how you presented yourself at Kinky Gerlinky and on the credits for Pam's shows. Why did you become "Winn"?

WINN: I didn't feel like my birth name described me. It didn't make me whole. I wanted a name that was fluid. When anyone asks me what my pronouns are, I just ask them what they see. I don't want to be put in a box. Who wants that? I just want people to understand me.

MARK: For a lot of people, particularly younger people, who declare themselves non-binary or who use the term "gender-fluid," it still seems important that they give it a name, to be part of a community.

WINN: Well, we didn't have these things when I was growing up. You were a drag queen or a transvestite, and the word transsexual wasn't used. I understand it's important for some people to label themselves, but it isn't for me. I just want to be treated how I expect to be treated. Call me whatever you want.

When I go home, my family might call me by my birth name and it never makes me feel uncomfortable, because these are people who have known me since I was a child—you can't be around someone for thirty or forty years and expect them to change the vocabulary they use overnight. They're not being malicious, and I'm not going to disregard their love because they call me a different name. The love I received as a child is the same love I receive as an adult. They've seen my work and admire it, they understand me, and I get a lot of respect from them because they can see the world is changing and opening up, and they know that a member of their family is thriving in that world.

MARK: There are similarities between your story and the DJ Honey Dijon's. You are both Black, transgender, and have had long careers in nightlife and fashion. You also both began as performers in clubs. She always says people see her color before they consider her gender, and she called one of her albums *Black Girl Magic*, which is a kind of manifesto for her. She rarely references having transitioned but is open to talking about it. How important are these kinds of definitions for you? I imagine a lot of Honey's audience don't even know she is transgender or, of course, care.

WINN: For each person it's different. I see myself as more genderqueer than transgender because labels don't appeal to me, and "queer" is a rejection of labels. "Winn Austin" has always existed, and as long you get who I am as a person, that's all that matters. My grandmother once told me, "Everybody can tell you they love you, but how many people can show you?"

MARK: Like Honey, you're also now designing and have your own label, Ms A, a collaboration with the illustrator and creative director Bok Goodall. What are the main differences between high street lingerie and Ms A, which is for transgender women?

WINN: Well, in womenswear I would be a size 10–12, but because of my build and my body length, I take a 12–14. Even if you fully transition, your body length may not be the same as other women's. And I need space to accommodate me physically in the crotch area. I have always had to work out how to look good on stage, without compromising on the aesthetic. I have never tape-tucked, ever. However, I have often bought lingerie from the 1950s, because the sizing is different and it accommodates me, which is why we've taken inspiration from that period for Ms A. This is about garments that are breathable and wearable. I don't believe style should come with discomfort.

MARK: The trans community comes under constant attack. It comes under literal attack from transphobic men, and it also faces egregious assaults from women who write transphobic opinions couched as gender critical feminism. As a highly visible trans individual, some people expect you to lead a fight against that. They want you to be Marsha P. Johnson, throwing bricks.

WINN: I didn't have the same experience that Marsha P. Johnson did growing up. I always had the security of my family, and if things went belly-up, I could always just go home. My reality has always been totally different from hers, and I operate in a different way.

When I was hanging out at Michael and Gerlinde's World store, which they opened opposite The Ivy in Covent Garden in 1988, I found that people liked and trusted me because I would show kindness and a generosity of spirit. When you're like that, people want to be around you.

Winn Austin at Bob Bob Ricard, London.
Bodysuit by Ms A; vintage tailcoat and boots by Vivienne Westwood.

MARK: The scene around World was all about mixing so many disparate elements. The stock was all personal to Michael and Gerlinde, from Native American and Brazilian headdresses to Keith Haring and Kenny Scharf pieces from New York, all of it picked up on their travels. World was fashion, drag, queer, gay, and straight. But a lot of the gay scene at the time didn't mix—it still doesn't. There's an internalized homophobia that manifests in its obsession with hypermasculinity in leather, military, and utility clothing—or indeed an absence of clothing and the display of musculature. There are still clubs that are men-only, and the people who run them would stop a gay man dressed as a woman entering their space as much as they would a transgender woman. A lot of those gay men, who are mostly white and middle-aged or older, would side with the gender critical feminists who really don't want to see an LGBTQ+ inclusive community.

WINN: If you don't want me in a place, it's not somewhere I want to be anyway. I was once thrown out of a men-only tent at the festival Summer Rites, and when they escorted me out of that tent I thought it was hilarious, because what it said to me was that they could see my femininity. When you grow up as a Black child, something like that means nothing to you. I can't change the color of my skin, and I can't change who I am.

When I first got to London, I was hanging out at Heaven, and although a lot of people there presented themselves as super-masculine, those people mentored me. I was working in the cloakroom, and I remember Dario who worked with me. He was a wonderful human. There were a lot of men who were a lot older than me who were clones, and delightful. I learnt about art history, music, and camp from them.

I do understand there is an aspect to the community that fixates on hypermasculinity. I used to go to the Coleherne, the gay pub in Earl's Court, on a Sunday. I'd mince in with my friend Neville, and the majority of people were nice, but you never went near the part of the bar close to the Brompton Road entrance—that was where the clientele was super-macho, with leather caps and harnesses and biker jackets. They had no motorcycle outside, but they had a certain attitude. They didn't interest me anyway.

MARK: When we were all going to Kinky Gerlinky, a lot of the people there were dressed in head-to-toe Vivienne Westwood. She used to go to the club, too, with her muse Sara Stockbridge. It was like a cult. Michael and Gerlinde had an impressive collection of McLaren and Westwood, and 178 full outfits ended up in the V&A permanent collection. I have never seen you as being aligned with a certain designer, even though you were friends with Rifat, Pam, and Nicholas Knightly.

WINN: I do have special pieces from designers that I cherish, including a lot of Vivienne Westwood, but I would never wear just one label. I used to go regularly to Kensington Market in the 1980s, and I have a rare John Crancher Pour L'Anarchie skirt. He was hugely influential, particularly for his bondage coats, with their straps and kilt detail, and he ran his own club nights. Like too many of his generation, he was taken from us by AIDS.

I have always had my own sense of style and know what suits me. I know what periods of fashion I like. I have never wanted to be current—I like bringing modernity to something from the past. No one wore floor-length evening dresses in the 1990s but me, and a lot of designers came to the club, saw that and took it to the catwalk.

I was always a stiletto heel girl. I still have the first pair I bought from Shellys. I admire glamorous Black women—Josephine Baker, Lena Horne, Diana Ross, Billie Holiday, Diahann Carroll, and my relatives. I've studied a lot about Black history and have always loved seeing Black women on album covers. All the most stylish women in Guyana looked like me, so I could relate. When I moved to London as a teenager, I knew what kind of Black person I wanted to be.

MARK: You prefer "transwoman of color" as a term rather than Black. Why is that?

WINN: Because I think it's more modern. By restricting myself to "Black," I am setting myself apart from a lot of my sisters elsewhere in the world.

MARK: London was still an aggressively racist environment when you arrived in 1980. What was your experience of that?

WINN: Well, I was aware of it. Even in Guyana I knew about the history of America, and the images of water hosing and setting dogs on people. In England, my experience was limited until I was assaulted by the police in the grounds of my home. We were living in a beautiful six-bedroom house in a predominantly white part of North London. I was roller-skating with my brother, and two drunk policemen assaulted us. They thought that we were trespassing. My stepfather and mother went to report the incident, and nothing came of it. But while I was aware of the house fire in New Cross in 1981, and the riots that followed in Brixton, I didn't live in that part of town, and while I knew it was unjust, I was just a child.

MARK: Your life changed when you became friends with Michael and Gerlinde. How did that come about?

WINN: It was through going to World. I didn't know who they were when I first started hanging out there. I didn't come to London with any fashion knowledge, but I got to know everyone who everyone else wanted to know. I made friends easily. World was a meeting place before social media existed. When I walked into that space, I felt so comfortable—it was like no other shop in the city. I met Scarlett, Roy, and Martin Confusion. Like Kensington Market, it was somewhere you'd spend the whole day.

MARK: Every Kinky Gerlinky event was documented on video by Dick Jewell, and his VHS cassettes that were sold at World were like early versions of Instagram. They were long recordings and, actually, profoundly boring. Most of it was just footage of people coming down the stairs into the club. I remember being on the Kinky Gerlinky coach trip to the Haçienda in Manchester for the party Michael and Gerlinde did with Paul Cons and Lucy Scher of Flesh, and they were screening them on the TV sets in the bus while we drove. We took a break at a service station and Leigh Bowery stood in the queue to pay for a Mars Bar, wearing his track pants with his pierced cheeks. It was so strange to be with all those people in the daytime, because it felt as if we shouldn't exist together outside of clubland. But the films are fascinating because they record that temporary world. They are Warholian in how banal they are, but you'd just keep watching to see yourself or your friends.

WINN: I didn't spend much time watching the videos because I had lived that life, but when friends who were younger and hadn't been part of that scene came over to my house, they wanted to watch the videos. They used to stay up to watch them all night. I would often wake up in the morning and hear my voice coming from the TV.

MARK: Michael and Gerlinde were so important in the history of London fashion, and you are still close friends with Michael, who has a presence in Dover Street Market. Michael has a long history with 430 Kings Road, the shop space McLaren and Westwood founded that's now Worlds End. He told me that he became a regular customer with Gerlinde when it was SEX in 1974. He remembers the first thing he bought: a transparent cerise skin-tight T-shirt, then a black "wet look" T-shirt, followed by apricot-colored Oxford bags tapered at the hem. Gerlinde used to go to the supermarket in her SEX rubber mac and rubber leggings with super-high black patent stilettos and studded ankle straps. The pair of them never had a division between the clothes they wore during the day and their nightlife wardrobe. Is that the same with you, or are there different Winns?

WINN: Well, I'd look ridiculous going to Tesco in a fake fur coat and maxi dress. But if I am coming home from an event, I'll pop into the 24-hour supermarket wearing that outfit and won't care. Clothing isn't the essence of me, but I like dressing up—it's my joy to transform myself in that way with wigs, jewelry, shoes, hats, heels and gloves. It brings me to life.

I must have been about four or five when it started. I lived with my grandmother. We were inseparable, very like-minded—both Scorpios. She used to allow me to do anything I wanted. I would dress up in her clothes and heels and pretend I was going shopping in the market. All the women in my family were glamorous, and church on a Sunday was the fashion show. Despite the heat in Guyana they would all wear gloves, capes, nets over the face, big hoop skirts. I see what I do as the same—I dress for the occasion. But I bring my essence no matter what I'm doing. If I go out in a tracksuit, I bring it. And you'll still recognize me, walking down the street in my strength.

Drop-waist fringed skirt and
double-breasted jacket by Ports
1961, *c.* late 2010s.

Gold stretch satin dress by
Jeffrey Bryant, 1991.

Black tulle dress by a student
at London College of Fashion,
unlabeled, *c.* late 2010s.

157

Cerise sequin suit by Rifat Ozbek,
Spring/Summer 1994.

Red velvet dress by
Tim Perkins, 1995.

159

Dress by
Grass-Fields,
c. late 2010s;
bracelets from
Top Shop, 1994.

160

Feather-trimmed black velvet dress
with matador-inspired red cape by
Tomasz Starzewski, *c.* early 2000s;
multicolored necklace from Lee's Mardi
Gras Boutique, New York; panther
clasp bracelet from Primark.

Bondage dress by
Pam Hogg, 1990.

Black sequin dress by
Jeffrey Bryant, 1991.

163

Vintage bias-cut 1930s-style
dress; cuffs by Erickson
Beamon, *c.* mid 2000s.

Chiffon jungle dress by
Jeffrey Bryant, 1992.

8 | Carmen Haid

Austrian-born Carmen Haid has been making significant things happen in fashion for over twenty years. A self-styled "vintage curator," with a skill set that combines a comprehensive knowledge of fashion history with how the industry works today, she is also a bona fide aesthete. Everyone in the industry knows her, and many turn to her for unaffected, honest counsel.

For long periods of her life in London, Paris, and Marrakech, she has been a high-profile exponent of that amorphous pursuit known as "fashion PR." She has worked with Yves Saint Laurent, Alber Elbaz, Hedi Slimane, and Tom Ford during their time at Yves Saint Laurent and with Michael Kors at Céline. Most notably, in an industry in which the role of PR often represents gatekeeping, Haid has excelled at brand communication. While fashion PR often divides designers from the media, she has bridged the two worlds in inventive and creative ways.

Haid has always celebrated the glamour of fashion. She appreciates extraordinary textiles and the craft of couture. In 2007, she launched Atelier-Mayer, Europe's first online boutique for luxury vintage fashion, and in 2022 she relaunched the brand with a focus on interiors and crafts from Morocco. Throughout her career she has amassed a remarkable amount of eveningwear and accessories by Saint Laurent, Céline, Lanvin, Balenciaga, Givenchy, Mugler, Christian Dior, Pierre Balmain, and other greats of Paris fashion from the twentieth century. Like her work, Haid's collection reflects her understanding of the power of clothes to accentuate a moment and bring joy, as well as their importance in social history, while she also retains a sense of perspective about what they are and the industry that generates them.

Carmen Haid at home in Marrakech.
Chiffon ensemble and embroidered belt by Yves Saint Laurent; earclips by Chanel; porcelain ring by Loulou de la Falaise; high heel sandals by Givenchy.

MARK: After I walked into your wardrobe in London and looked at all the brocade and velvet, I was able to say without any doubt at all who it all belonged to. What do you think the common denominator is?

CARMEN: It is a certain kind of eveningwear. Right now, we live in a time that is defined by streetwear, and that's a reflection of our lives and lifestyle. It's all about comfort and versatility, easy clothing, rather than elaborate fabrics. Fundamentally, that's why I like eveningwear textiles so much—because it takes time to create a beautiful piece of cloth and an exquisite garment. I like to wear and collect these because it's honoring and celebrating craftsmanship, which makes me happy.

MARK: There always seems to be a story with the way you put things together. Whereas a certain energy is absent from streetwear, and there's certainly no depth of emotion in fast fashion, your clothes have a resonance to them.

CARMEN: We live in a time where one outfit must do everything for you. You need to go from the gym to work to cocktails. Plus, you have to blend in at the office, or wherever your workplace is. Do we still have Casual Friday? I don't think it exists anymore. Essentially, everything is casual now—it's all about comfort. The whole idea of what dressing entails has changed. But eveningwear is for an occasion. It has beauty, mystery, and glamour.

MARK: Your collection has a timeless feel to it. There's not a lot that reflects a trend from any particular time, although the silhouettes of certain things were obviously more popular in certain eras than others—like a lot of flowing pieces that conjure up Talitha Getty in Morocco, and certain 1960s pieces that have the essence of retrofuturism. Is that because you primarily buy vintage?

CARMEN: The kind of fashion I love is about expressing a dream—the opulence and the night-time, but also the freedom to mix and match different colors and materials. It invites the imagination. I want to put something on to feel good, elevated, transported. Vintage can be so beautiful—you just need a couple of things to mix with your contemporary wardrobe, and it immediately becomes unique.

MARK: Which designer appears most in your collection? I'm guessing it's Yves Saint Laurent, partly because of your history with the house.

CARMEN: Correct. I was working with Monsieur Saint Laurent, initially as a press assistant, from 1996 when he was still designing both collections—haute couture and prêt-à-porter. Then he retired to focus purely on the couture, and Alber Elbaz was hired for womenswear and Hedi Slimane to look after menswear. Neither were well known back then. I remember it all seemed so new. At the first Hedi Slimane show there were no more than thirty journalists in attendance, and Alber's first collection wasn't received with the greatest applause either. It's astonishing to me to think how that changed, when three seasons later the brand was sold to the Gucci group—now Kering—and Tom Ford moved from Gucci to YSL to become creative director for both men and women.

MARK: There were periods before Saint Laurent passed the baton on when the brand had been diluted to the point of irrelevance. I bought a pair of trainers for about £20 in Brixton Market at some point in the 1990s, and they were so obviously the product of what happens when a brand licenses itself to anyone with a budget. They were so kitsch, almost like one of those Chanel guillotine sculptures by Tom Sachs. They had the YSL logo on, and they may have been the product of a legitimate license, but they were like a visual joke. You could also buy Yves Saint Laurent cigarettes for a long time. That kind of licensing was so lowbrow. It was all about the application of "class" to something that was just terrible product.

CARMEN: Well, actually, when Tom Ford took over at Yves Saint Laurent, that was seen as a disaster by many. The sentiment was essentially "How can an American take over the fashion heritage of France?" *Le Monde* and *Le Figaro* were scathing. But he stayed and gradually managed to initiate a necessary change, including the management.

I continued to work with Tom for a while, and it became an exciting time for the Gucci Group because they were scooping up so many brands. We had a memo every week about a new acquisition—Bottega Veneta, Alexander McQueen in 2000, Stella McCartney a year later. LVMH was doing the same—Céline became a part of the group in 1996 and Michael Kors became creative director a year after. I worked with Michael for five years and his collections had an indication of what was later to become a signature at his own line, casual *de luxe*.

MARK: It must have been fascinating to work alongside Yves Saint Laurent and his successors, but what appealed to you about the actual product?

CARMEN: Those clothes reflect my style more than any others. I love the blend of colors and materials, the elegance and feminine power, the strength and seduction, the use of paisley and the inspiration from his travels. Yves Saint Laurent was so radical and such a rebel—he was the first to feature Black models in his fashion shows and he photographed himself naked for his perfume campaign. He gave women power in the form of perfectly tailored jackets and suits. Le Smoking was born in 1962 and is still one of the most elegant codes to wear. You put a single piece of his clothing on and instantly feel chic.

MARK: I remember going to see the huge retrospective at the Petit Palais in 2010, two years after Saint Laurent died, and then the inaugural show at the Musée Yves Saint Laurent in 2017, which really made me rethink the brand in a big way. He was so radical for so much of his career. Alicia Drake's book *The Beautiful Fall* (2006), about the competition and relationship between him and Lagerfeld and that whole fast set in 1970s Paris, is one of the best books about the industry ever written. He was wild. What do you think was at the core of his magic?

CARMEN: I bought a beautiful red floral Yves Saint Laurent chiffon dress that belonged to Loulou de la Falaise [page 183]. I met her several times, and I asked her once what she thought was the secret to his success. She believed that it was all to do with him focusing on dressing the people around him, his friends. Today, fashion is a lot about dressing for the red carpet and influencers that a designer has never actually met. It is a financial transaction, not necessarily a relationship. Saint Laurent's personality shone through his relationships. Loulou was incredibly significant to him, a true muse.

MARK: You have a lot of pieces from the *Opéras – Ballets Russes* collection from 1976 [pages 176–177]. Why is that such a significant season in the YSL canon?

CARMEN: I love the detail, the sumptuous colors of the velvets, the trimmings and silhouettes, which were taken from Russian Cossacks. The *Opéras – Ballets Russes* collection was an homage to Sergei Diaghilev's Ballets Russes—Yves Saint Laurent was very interested in Russian culture, especially in Léon Bakst's costumes for Diaghilev's Russian seasons in Paris. This "byzantine luxury look," as it was dubbed by the French press, would remain for many more seasons to come. It is still more than relevant for eveningwear today.

MARK: Where did your obsession with eveningwear come from?

CARMEN: From my late grandmother, Klaudia Mayer, who was a haute couture seamstress in Austria at the turn of the century, during the Vienna Secession art movement that included the work of Egon Schiele, Gustav Klimt, Josef Hoffmann, and Koloman Moser. I spent many summers at my grandmother's house and in her atelier, draping fabrics and dressing my Barbie dolls. That was my first experience of fashion, and it's where my love for eveningwear stems from, because my grandmother worked on many pieces with incredible couture fabrics. I named my Atelier-Mayer brand in tribute to her, and I wanted to celebrate the tradition of "*les petites mains*," a French term referring to the highly skilled craftspeople who execute haute couture designs.

Carmen Haid at home in Maida Vale, London.
Brocade jacket by Koos Van Den Akker; blouse by Caroline Charles;
harem pants by Yves Saint Laurent; shoes by Christian Louboutin.

MARK: And when did you start arranging things with the intention of a collection?

CARMEN: I was immersed in it from a young age. I started at around three years old when my mother took me to flea markets and thrift shops. At one point I had over 1,000 pieces, including accessories—a lot of vintage Chanel, Schiaparelli, Christian Dior, and YSL jewelry, but also incredible unsigned designer pieces I found on the side of the road in house clearance sales.

I was always naturally drawn to vintage—it excites me and supports my philosophy of modern fashion. The world is overproducing. Repurposing is the way forward—it's about recycling in a chic way, which is what I did with the first iteration of Atelier-Mayer. It started as an online business, because I wanted to reach a global audience to spread the word of vintage and never wanted an actual store. However, we had clients who wanted a physical experience, so we ended up having a private client showroom, pop-ups in department stores, and private trunk shows all over the world. We shipped to more than 100 countries and had a warehouse at London Bridge. I was on a mission to educate people about repurposing hand-crafted work in places where it's not necessarily available. It felt exciting and creative. I developed an augmented retail app with Holition, which we launched during the *FT How to Spend it* Luxury of Business conference in Vienna in 2013. I also produced a magazine, so that as well as the online material there was something tangible we could give to customers to keep and which would inspire them. It became a collector's item—we sold it at Colette Paris and Dover Street Market, and it was also a supplement to the *Vanity Fair* Hollywood issue.

MARK: I'm interested in the stories behind some of the pieces in your collection, like the YSL dress that belonged to Loulou de la Falaise. What resonance does a dress like that have for you?

CARMEN: We are all vibrational beings. All materials in existence are, from a scientific point of view, in motion. When you have a piece of clothing that has been worn by someone that you admire or have loved, it resonates. You remember a good time that you had while wearing a certain piece of clothing, and while you can't explain it, it transmits a feeling. With the YSL dress, I was instinctively drawn to it. I love the colors and texture, and of course it was personal to Loulou de la Falaise, which to me makes it special. I have also been known to feng shui clothing to bring back the equilibrium to its original form.

MARK: If Yves Saint Laurent is your all-time favorite designer, who comes second?

CARMEN: Thierry Mugler was up there—the way the jackets were nipped in at the waist, with the power shoulders. I also love Azzedine Alaïa, André Courrèges, Pierre Balmain, Givenchy, Arnold Scaasi, Halston, Bill Blass, Valentino, Nina Ricci, Guy Laroche, Thea Porter, and Zandra Rhodes. But for me, the designer I would rate as a close second to Saint Laurent is Paco Rabanne, because of how completely radical he was. His work belonged to the space-age era in the 1960s, when everyone was trying to envision what the year 2000 would look like. That futuristic vision appears in so many of his designs from the era. It is minimal, clean, and incredibly well done.

MARK: So many designers from that era tapped into that spirit, including Pierre Cardin and Courrèges. Now we live in the future that they were projecting on to, and everyone is wearing sweatpants. I feel a degree of "we were promised jetpacks" disappointment—how about you?

CARMEN: Actually, they were prescient to foresee masks and face coverings, and clothing with minimal and functional design. The idea of the space age revolved around the idea of exploration, of pushing boundaries further than ever before—whether that meant with technology, materials, or silhouettes—and this is still the case today.

MARK: I think a lot of what was happening in that period was down to the fact that the year 2000 was distant but in view. For a lot of those designers, they were creating for a year that they felt sure they would live to see, and yet the number just sounded so far removed from where they were at the time. Now we've passed it, so we aren't looking forward as much. The year 3000 is a fantasy—none of us will be here for it.

CARMEN: The only thing we need to think about, going forward, is how to save our planet and what we can contribute by being more sustainable in every aspect of our lives. There's no date in the calendar we need to consider because climate change is already telling us what the situation is. We are evolving fast. Look at *Blade Runner*, which seemed so futuristic in 1982. Uber has a flying car now, we have the metaverse, we use FaceTime on our phones, and Amazon uses robots to deliver products. It's all just as the film predicted.

What I love most is when something mixes futuristic technology and craft, which is why I love those retro space-age designs so much. And I like how that translates into all things experiential—like when you walk into a Stella McCartney store and it smells of fresh mountain air and there's a living green wall, or maybe you buy a coat that has heat-generating technology. The VR headset currently resembles a space-age creation but I'm sure that soon it will look like a sleek pair of sunglasses, just as the first mobile phone was a brick in comparison to today's smartphones.

MARK: How much craft and technique has become extinct over the decades? Your collection is a showcase of specialist workmanship and textiles as much as anything.

CARMEN: Certainly, some of the resins used in the accessories aren't employed anymore, and a lot of the brocades and velvets are uncommon today—which is a pity because they are so beautiful. The shine on some of my brocades is close to psychedelic. Wools are quite different today too, and of course we won't be seeing much fur at all in the future.

MARK: How do you feel about that? It seems as if all the major houses decided to stop using it simultaneously.

CARMEN: It's the way forward. I am not an advocate of fur, but I do have vintage pieces and love them. I also have contemporary faux fur jackets. I don't believe in killing animals whatsoever—however, the vintage furs already exist, so what can you do? Burn them?

MARK: There's currently a debate in the industry over the longevity of fur as a material, and how synthetic alternatives aren't sustainable and often use harsh chemicals in production. But the fashion conglomerates will dictate the future, of course, and that decision will be driven by what they think is most appealing to the largest group of consumers, rather than any moral compass. Glossing over ethics for a moment, who do you think created the most interesting pieces using fur in the past?

CARMEN: Undoubtedly, Oscar de la Renta. I have a fabulous mink bomber jacket of his from the 1970s. Elsa Schiaparelli, Dior, and Vionnet were also wonderful. I think they were special because most of the design was done by furriers working with them, not the design houses themselves. It was such a specialist craft and so niche. When you look at fur jackets from the 1930s, you will see the client's initials stitched inside the lining, because they were made purely for that individual. Which is something we are seeing more of now—personalization in high fashion, though not necessarily couture. But fur is really finished. On a few occasions when I was dealing in vintage, I had people bringing me pieces in monkey fur, and of course I couldn't touch it. You can go to prison for that. I had a leopard skin coat from 1974 that didn't have any kind of paperwork so it couldn't be sold on. I am not going to wear a real leopard skin, so I turned it into a stool and made neck rolls out of the sleeves. I made sure we didn't waste a single inch of that beautiful animal.

MARK: I'd like to talk about one of the oldest pieces in your collection—the black velvet Paul Poiret opera gown with the brocade detail, which is from the early 1900s [**page 187**]. It feels much more like a museum piece, and like costume, than fashion. Poiret isn't a name that has been traded on in the twenty-first century, but of course he is well known to fashion academics, designers, and historians. It's a piece that feels like an anomaly in your wardrobe. What drew you to it?

CARMEN: Poiret was designing textiles as well as gowns, and he spent a lot of time researching in Vienna during the Secession movement, before taking that back to his studio in Paris. It was the time of oversized coats and opera gowns, and he perfected them. If you look at the detail on the button on that robe, it is simple but exquisite. It's one big button, one big coat. That's a principle that still works today.

Poiret's work was modernity expressed through the structural simplicity of clothing, signifying a pivotal movement in the emergence of Modernism. There was a fabulous exhibition, *Poiret: King of Fashion*, at the Met in 2007. I love the work that he was immersed in—Egon Schiele and Gustav Klimt. It's such a part of my aesthetic. I based the look of my kitchen in London on Klimt. Josef Hoffmann was an architect, but he also did polka dots in 1900—he was the Damien Hirst of his time.

MARK: Saint Laurent changed fashion forever, particularly with the introduction of prêt-à-porter as the industry's standard model. Subsequently, the designer was perceived as a kind of mythical figure. Who rode the wave of that change?

CARMEN: I appreciate creatives who capture the cultural zeitgeist of the day. Since Saint Laurent, the visionaries have been Karl Lagerfeld, who was a genius of capturing the mood of the moment for decades, Alexander McQueen for challenging the traditional concept of catwalk, Stella McCartney for being a pioneer of sustainability in business, Vivienne Westwood for being an activist by creating disruptive clothing to provoke social and political change, Rei Kawakubo for her iconoclastic vision, and Hussein Chalayan for his experimental and innovative designs, in particular his 2000 *After Words* collection, with the wooden table that turned into a skirt.

Currently, I am interested in Daniel Roseberry, Alessandro Michele, Gabriela Hearst and Kim Jones, as well several friends of mine who have all interesting smaller fashion brands, such as Huishan Zhang—who embraces his Chinese roots—and Christopher Raeburn, with his concept of reworking surplus fabrics.

There is still so much to look at today that has the same radical attitude as the early twentieth century. Fashion remains an endless source of inspiration and innovation. I am excited about the integration of technology more and more into everyday living, as well as blending it with the senses, understanding the psychology of color in clothing, and consumer behavior. Innovative and sustainable materials will create the fashion of the future, but we can still cherish craftsmanship and heritage.

Harem pants, blouse, and crochet hat by Yves Saint Laurent, *Opéras – Ballets Russes* collection, Autumn/Winter 1976; bolero jacket by Yves Saint Laurent, Autumn/Winter 1975.

Brocade dress by Eisa
(Cristóbal Balenciaga), 1959;
minaudière *c.* 1940s; Chanel
Haute Couture pearl and
diamanté earclips, *c.* 1950s.

Cotton dress by Yves Saint Laurent, *c.* 1970s; earclips by Elsa Schiaparelli, *c.* 1950s.

179

Chiffon dress by
Céline, *c.* 1970s.

Hand-embroidered
jacket by Halston,
1978; harem pants by
Yves Saint Laurent,
1979; one of a kind
diamanté leopard print
bag by Celine, *c.* 1970s.

Chiffon ensemble by Yves Saint Laurent, 1977, from the collection of Loulou de la Falaise; Indian turquoise and ruby flower bracelet, *c.* 1970s.

Chiffon and gold brocade
dress by Pauline Trigère,
c. 1960s.

Hand-embroidered brocade kaftan, unsigned, *c.* 1960s; silk chiffon turban, Christian Dior Haute Couture, 1974.

Dress and jacket with mink
detail by Christian Dior, 1967.

Velvet and brocade
opera coat with mother
of pearl buttons, Paul
Poiret, *c.* 1930s.

Evening gown by Christian
Dior Couture, *c.* 1970s;
headband by Chanel, *c.* 1990s.

189

9 | Susanne Bartsch

For more than four decades the Swiss-born entrepreneur, artist, and performer Susanne Bartsch has been a creative force for change in New York fashion and club culture. In 1981, after thirteen years in London, she moved into the historic Chelsea Hotel on West 23rd Street in New York and has remained in residence ever since. She was instrumental in the early success of John Galliano, Stephen Jones, BodyMap, and numerous other British designers, bringing global attention to them through shows staged in New York and Tokyo. She also sold their work at her Bartsch Boutique.

In 1987, she began hosting the weekly party Savage (next to the Chelsea Hotel). This was followed by Bentley's and then the Copacabana, which ran until 1993. Since 1989, she has raised over $2.5m for AIDS charities with her international Love Ball nights and continued to create major events in her adopted city, hosting nights at Le Bain and the Boom Boom Room at the Standard High Line, Bartschland Follies at McKittrick Hotel, and dance parties at Elsewhere in Brooklyn. Her Halloween events have been a highlight of the nightlife calendar for decades, and in 2018 she was the subject of the documentary *Susanne Bartsch: On Top*.

In 2022, she debuted her Bartschland capsule collection at New York Fashion Week as part of her Look event showcasing six young designers: Casey Caldwell, Dope Tavio, Guvanch, Jessica Jade, Kim Mesches, and Sho Konishi. Her influence on New York culture and international fashion was explored in detail in the 2015 FIT exhibition *Fashion Underground: The World of Susanne Bartsch*, featuring over 120 looks from her archive, including one-off pieces by The Blonds, Leigh Bowery, Thierry Mugler, and Mister Pearl.

Susanne Bartsch at the Chelsea Hotel, New York.
Shorts and jacket by Jean Paul Gaultier; boots by Zaldy.

MARK: Nightlife involves many rituals, and I see the most significant one as getting ready to go out. Does that resonate for you?

SUSANNE: Absolutely. I love the ritual of picking out an outfit and working out what goes with what. I have been wearing a rhinestone-encrusted Kyle Farmery bodysuit from his Sparkyle Studio recently, and when I put it on, I feel like the Bionic Woman. I have great legs and it accentuates them. I love that you can wear it so many different ways. A friend gave me some long-fringed gloves, which turned it into a kind of saloon cowboy look.

MARK: Whenever I have been with you at the Chelsea, there always seem to be a lot of people coming and going. Is getting ready also an important social ritual for you? Sue Tilley, who always spent hours with Leigh Bowery and Trojan dressing up before they went to Taboo, has said that the most enjoyable part of any night was the time before they actually left the flat, when they were applying makeup, drinking, and gossiping. The concept and the ritual were more important than the actual club, and the club was really just a pretext.

SUSANNE: I do like to have people around when I'm getting ready. Deney Adam comes to do my makeup, and we have friends over. Preparing to go out now takes longer and has become a more involved ritual, because my makeup and hair and wigs have got bigger. It's drag. I am always in drag!

My looks fall into three categories: day drag, semi-drag, and full drag. Day drag is maybe some vintage Gaultier and a little makeup and a ponytail hair piece. Semi involves heavier makeup, wigs, and bigger heels, and full drag is head to toe looks. Dressing up is a form of self-expression. To me, it's like going to the doctor—it's therapy, including the work that goes into creating the drag. It's all part of a process.

MARK: Why have drag and nightlife always gone hand in hand?

SUSANNE: Because if you are creating a persona, and you're spending all that time dressing up and perfecting a look, then there's no point doing it unless you can show it off. It's like dressing up for Christmas dinner, it's a celebration, and it doesn't actually achieve its potential unless you have the meal together.

MARK: So the event itself is crucial, like dressing up to go to a fashion show even though you're in the audience and not actually a part of what's being presented. It's visual communication and it's nuanced. But the nature of preparation for an event has changed since you started hosting parties, just as both nightlife and fashion shows exist and unfold in real time beyond the space where they are happening. The preparation and the unveiling of your look, as you walk down the hallway at the Chelsea Hotel on your way out, is always live on social media.

SUSANNE: It has certainly changed the way I dress. I can't wear the same thing twice now. Even though the image is fleeting, it's been documented, so I can't post the same outfit three days after I first wore it. It has to be totally different. That's why the styling has changed so much and become so much more involved—it makes you see the clothing in a totally different way. I can spend a lot of time on an extraordinary wig, and it transforms a dress.

MARK: Has technology worked for or against you?

SUSANNE: We've learned how to use it. When the pandemic hit in 2020, nightlife was the first thing to close down and all my friends, including Amanda Lepore and Joey Arias, were suddenly out of work. So we held Zoom parties. That saved us. Those parties kept me sane. I dressed up, and we worked out a revenue stream with people paying to join in, so that meant my people could eat. I learned how to communicate via a screen, like getting 800 people to show their boobs on camera all at once.

MARK: Using the internet to connect socially is antithetical to the way nightlife works, but the pandemic was an extreme situation that forced us to find ways to stay connected. That aside, our digital lives have made us more connected than ever before, but also more isolated.

SUSANNE: Yes, social media has taken away from the moment. There are lots of positive elements but so many downsides. It is tacky and cheap. People compare themselves with other people, and it's fake. I could be an eighteen-year-old boy on Instagram. There's no more underground, because within a second something is broadcast around the world.

One of the only things that still works is dancing: the dancefloor, the music, and people being in the moment together. We move differently, but to the same beat. It's great to see that. I like it when I look at the dancefloor and no one has their phone out.

MARK: Your fashion roots are more in London than New York. Tell me about your history with the city and what it means to you in terms of fashion.

SUSANNE: London is where I got to know so many people who shaped my life, like Ossie Clark, and Michael and Gerlinde Costiff, who were my closest friends. I moved to London from Switzerland in the late 1960s and fashion went through huge changes while I lived there. My boyfriend at the time, Paul Reeves, owned The Universal Witness, which was part of a radical movement that put men in floral shirts, velvet, and satin pants for the first time in the twentieth century. I met David Bowie at his store. Then Tommy Roberts opened Mr Freedom in Chelsea in 1969, and his work had an immediate impact on streetstyle—everyone had a pair of velvet dungarees from that store and rainbow cropped wraparound knit jackets.

There was also Alkasura, from 1967 until the mid-1970s, which Paul originally founded with John Lloyd, who then ran it alone after Paul went his own way in 1969. Vern Lambert was an important figure at the time—he was a fashion historian who had a stall in the Chelsea Antiques Market selling pieces by Fortuny and Paul Poiret. He was Anna Piaggi's companion and collaborated with her for years. He moved to Milan in the 1970s to live with her and went on to work with Karl Lagerfeld, and I took over his stall. He also gave me his apartment in Cheyne Walk, above Manolo Blahnik's store. Vern had an encyclopedic knowledge of fashion.

MARK: And then, of course, you took a lot of that energy to New York. It was interesting when a portfolio of photographs by Lucien Samaha surfaced on his Instagram account in 2022, documenting the opening of your second store in 1985 on West Broadway. I hadn't seen anything from that evening, but if that opening was today, it would flood my feed. Your two shops, and your work with the 1980s generation of designers from London, created a revolution in New York, and propelled those designers forward. How did it all come about?

SUSANNE: When I came to New York, for love, on Valentine's Day in 1981, I was leaving behind a lot. The New Romantic scene was a big deal, and so was the Blitz club, where everyone had a new look every Tuesday. In New York, fashion wasn't as interesting. People looked nice, but I missed the constantly changing looks and the dynamism. A friend suggested I import what I was missing. I saw a little shop space in SoHo, at 72 Thompson Street, called the number on the window, explained to the guy what I wanted to do and that I didn't have a big budget—that will be on my gravestone, by the way, "I don't have a big budget"—and he rented it to me for a good rate.

London fashion at the time was incredibly inventive but buyers weren't going. I brought over David Holah and his brother Eric's designs, made under their Nocturne label, and hats by Stephen Jones. I was selling jewelry by Andrew Logan and Dinny Hall. Michael Costiff came, stayed with me at the Chelsea for a while, and worked his magic to create the interior. John Duka, who was a fashion journalist at the time, and who later set up the PR company KCD, wrote a whole page on it for the *New York Times*. He was the first person to use the term "street fashion." Norma Kamali and Donna Karan used to visit for inspiration.

MARK: It was a bigger scene than just a store though—you were an agent for these designers as well as a retailer.

SUSANNE: I had a show at the Roxy in 1983, *New London in New York*, with Stephen Jones, Richard Torry, Leigh Bowery and Trojan, Rachel Auburn—one of the most underrated designers of that era—and BodyMap, which David Holah had gone on to launch with Stevie

Susanne Bartsch at the Chelsea Hotel, New York.
Woolen stole by Zaldy.

Stewart after they graduated from college. I set up a showroom and acted as their agent. I took $750,000 worth of orders, but the kids couldn't afford to produce it all. And suddenly I found myself running eighteen businesses.

That show was chaos, but everyone was on a massive high from it. Fashion people in New York were so used to everything being slick, like Calvin Klein, and it wasn't that at all. But it was inspiring.

I did two more shows at the Limelight—the first that same year and then the second in 1984—as well as one in Tokyo, which was an invitation by *WWD Japan*. Then I wanted to go back to basics and just have a shop again, so I stripped back what I was doing. Michael Costiff came back over to create another interior, and we opened a bigger space in 1985, stocking Judy Blame, Joe Casely-Hayford, and John Galliano before they were really known. But the guy who was backing me got done for insider trading, and I was thrown to the dogs. Peter Gatien from Limelight tried to help me, but that was going to involve a bank loan with huge interest. Then Annie Flanders from *Details* introduced me to someone who invested, but that ended badly too. They were trying to get me to sell cheap T-shirts and change the direction of the store, so I walked out. It stayed open for a few months after I left but then collapsed.

MARK: It's interesting that you mention John Duka as instrumental in the early success of the first store. It's widely believed that he was the basis for the character of Felix Turner in Larry Kramer's play about the AIDS epidemic, *The Normal Heart*. Felix is a lifestyle writer at the *New York Times* who—unwillingly at first, because he is in the closet at work—plays an instrumental role in bringing the virus to the mainstream media. There's dialogue in the play from Felix that really sums up the era, and the stigma and shame that forged homophobia with AIDS: "I just write about gay designers and gay discos and gay chefs and gay rock stars and gay photographers and gay models and gay celebrities and gay everything. I just don't call them gay." According to his colleagues Duka was openly gay at *New York* magazine, then moved to the *New York Times* in 1979 where he was guarded about his sexuality, went on to marry a woman, and died in 1989 from an AIDS-related illness, just before he turned forty. It was a tragic story of life and death in that decade, and in a way defined much of the era. He passed away the same year as Alvin Ailey, Robert Mapplethorpe, and Cookie Mueller. Tens of thousands of people had already died but the government response in the US was still pitiful. You held your first Love Ball fundraiser for AIDS at Roseland that year.

SUSANNE: I just had to do something. That first Love Ball came out of a dark place. We were all suffering in New York. We had lost so many people—every day someone else was gone. It had been terrifying. When Klaus Nomi was in hospital in 1982, we had to wear a hazmat suit to go and see him. No one knew what it was.

After so much pain, I decided I was going to fight, and do something that was constructive and raised money, but also awareness, and which celebrated life, both the lives of the people that had gone, and those still with us. It was based on the Harlem house balls I'd been going to for years. We did a second one in 1991, and an anniversary event in 2019. There was also La Balade de L'Amour at the Folies Bergères in Paris in 1992, where Gaultier and Mugler exchanged jackets on stage, and Azzedine Alaïa carried Jean-Paul Goude on his shoulders. Then we did The Hoppening in 1994 at the Playboy Mansion with Hugh Hefner, which raised over $600,000—Dita von Teese was there, before she was famous, and the model Heather Sweet was The Bondage Bunny, wearing a leather corset by Abel Villarreal. I was also very involved with the Life Ball in Vienna.

That first Love Ball was so important—it was the fashion community coming together to acknowledge we were all part of the epidemic. Madonna showed up, there was Anna Wintour and Isaac Mizrahi, Leigh Bowery, and Pepper LaBeija of House of LaBeija, Avis Pendavis, Willi Ninja, Jose Xtravaganza, and so many other legends. The proceeds of that night—$450,000—were distributed through DIFFA [Design Industries Foundation Fighting AIDS]. It was important to me and my committee that the money went to hands-on organizations, like God's Love We Deliver. We bought them a new van so that they could distribute more meals.

MARK: This industry has lost so many people, particularly to AIDS. Do you associate certain clothes you've kept with certain individuals? Do you keep things that you think are valuable?

SUSANNE: Not really. I have a lot of clothes, both at the Chelsea and in a storage unit in Brooklyn, but I'm not into the idea of possessions for monetary value. Certain wigs remind me of Gerlinde because we bought them when we were shopping together. And I miss her all the time. But mostly things bring me joy, like looking at a certain disco look I wore at the Delano in Miami on New Year's Eve. I try not to remember sad things.

There are things I wished I didn't get rid of—some 1920s beaded dresses and chiffon pieces from London. But I don't put a value on things, even though they might be worth a lot of money. I really like the idea of living in a hotel, so that I could leave any day on a whim. But that's obviously pure fantasy because I have so much stuff.

MARK: What's amazing is that, unlike a lot of people who have kept clothes from their past, you can fit into everything. I have kept a lot of the clubwear I had in the 1980s and 1990s which I'll never fit into again, but you're the same size as you were when you left London. Do you consciously maintain that for the clothes?

SUSANNE: It maintains itself. I don't take drugs or drink too much. It's probably genetic. I go to the gym, and I love to hate it. It makes me feel good, and if you feel good, then you look good.

MARK: How much does sex figure as part of your persona?

SUSANNE: I love sex. I'd call my style body-conscious. I can feel sexy in anything. I like short things and showing my legs off—a pair of Westwood heels will give you some oomph. I also like corsets. I love things that are restrictive because they make you feel a certain way. It's why I've always liked Mister Pearl for his corsetry. I have five or six of his pieces—in fact, I think I was his first client [**pages 202 and 207**]. His work makes you feel so glamorous and femme fatale. It is pure couture perfection. That craftsmanship has an energy that can't be paralleled.

MARK: Even though you say you aren't sentimental about clothing, I know you were devastated, as many were, by Manfred Mugler's passing in 2022. He was such a large presence in your life and work. Your close friend Joey Arias was his muse, and you got married to David Barton in a Mugler creation. How does looking at that dress make you feel now?

SUSANNE: I am still in shock. He touched us all. I have the most incredible memories. I was an Angel guinea pig and modeled for him. He came to my parties, and I always loved seeing him having a twirl.

When I first walked into FIT for my exhibition back in 2015, each piece evoked something. Having those clothes hidden away in your wardrobe is one thing but seeing them spotlighted on a mannequin in a gallery is another. The wedding dress by Manfred was a major moment for me. He created it to be tongue in cheek—he wanted me to look naked, wearing the bouquet on my head. It was whimsical. David and I had decided to get married at short notice, so Manfred collaborated via phone from Paris with Abel Villarreal in LA to put the piece together. Manfred was a total genius. The exhibition of his work in Montréal and Paris before he died was fabulous. People say he had a renaissance in the last ten years, but I don't think he ever stopped being an inspiration. His patterns and craftsmanship, and his visual representation of women, were groundbreaking. His work was timeless.

Catsuit and tulle
boa by David
Dalrymple, 2018.

Coat by Leigh
Bowery, 1983;
head piece by
Casey Caldwell,
Riot Wear
collection, 2013.

Body and skirt by
Mister Pearl, 1989.

202

Samurai jacket, obi belt,
and headpiece by
Mathu & Zaldy, 1995.

Coat by Vivienne Westwood,
Mini-Crini collection,
Spring/Summer 1985.

Dress by Vivienne
Westwood, *Mini-Crini*
collection, Spring/
Summer 1985.

Corset by The
Blonds, 2011;
headpiece by Luis
Payne, 2015.

206

Kewpie face doll dress
by Mister Pearl, 1985.

207

Dress and headpiece by
Mathu & Zaldy, c. 1989.

Dress by John Galliano,
Forgotten Innocents collection,
Autumn/Winter 1986.

10 | Karlo Steel

New York City has had an uneasy relationship with avant-garde fashion. Always a sideshow to Paris and Milan, but more commercially focused than London, New York's runway shows sit at a distance from its retail, which has always been conservative. The future of bricks and mortar internationally is uncertain, and the death of heavyweight high fashion department store Barneys—as well as the demise of several forward-thinking smaller stores faced with impossible rents and online competition—does nothing to suggest there will be a renaissance in Manhattan or elsewhere. But over the decades, the mere existence of certain retailers has helped change tastes in the city, if not the founder's fortunes.

The stylist and creative director Karlo Steel opened Atelier in 2002. Originally from New Orleans, he worked in retail in San Francisco in the 1990s before moving to New York at the end of the decade. For just over thirteen years his store championed a groundbreaking, predominantly European aesthetic, stocking artisanal and hard-to-source brands including Carol Christian Poell, Luca Laurini's Label Under Construction, and Maurizio Amadei's M.A+ as well as the Japanese masters Yohji Yamamoto and Comme des Garçons, and the all-black visions of Rick Owens and Ann Demeulemeester.

Karlo Steel at 130 Willliam, New York.
Coat by Yohji Yamamoto Pour Homme; sweater by Uniqlo.

MARK: I remember going to the first Atelier store on Crosby Street, and then the larger one on Hudson. Both had a mood that you rarely find in retail anymore, especially not in New York. It was serious. But then the construction of the clothes on display was serious. That was how things were until you sold the store in 2013 and moved on. Today the current Atelier still sells Yohji and Comme, but now also stocks Canada Goose. What happened?

KARLO: I think it was partly the rise of sportswear. That, and the parallel rise of digital, which flattened, atomized, and legitimized everything. I'm not saying that's a bad thing, it's just a different thing. The Atelier I opened belongs to a different era, and discretion in fashion doesn't have the same merit now.

MARK: A lot of things that were rarefied then are now mainstream. I walked through Shoreditch recently and there was a huge billboard with the Comme des Garçons Play heart logo on it, which is so far removed from what Comme was when it first appeared in Europe in the 1980s. Do you see this as diluting design?

KARLO: I don't think commerciality is a bad word. It's a delicate dance. Without business there is no art—and that's art with a small "a." I think it's a grave mistake to treat one's business as art. You have to build a reputation first.

Look at Rick Owens, who we stocked at Atelier, and who remained pure for a long time. Now he is doing collaborations with Dr. Martens and Birkenstocks, and I love it. It's great to make that aesthetic as mass as possible. We know what he is about, there is a vast body of work there to back it up, and now it's time to play with it. Where do you go after minimalism? There are two options: minimal-plus or maxi-minimalism. Rick is exploring minimal-plus.

MARK: Collaborations in fashion have become an instant way to generate social media attention, but a lot of them seem poorly thought out, and often the collaboration does little for either party involved. I'm interested in the collaborations you did with designers at Atelier, which were low-key and respectful of each of the designers you worked with. How did those come about, and what were your favorite pieces?

KARLO: We did two collaborations, one with YSL and another with Dior Homme. Rick Owens graciously did a mini collection for us, but it wasn't a collaboration. With YSL, Stefano Pilati came into our Hudson location and really liked what he saw. He connected with our vision and proposed the collaboration. Of course, I was over the moon that Atelier would be able to work with one of the most storied houses ever.

With Dior Homme, I made the proposition. There was a period under Kris Van Assche where he introduced an unstructured and fluid look. That resonated with me. It felt fresh after so many years of strictness.

MARK: It's increasingly rare that someone develops a unique aesthetic and a label that carries through every season. Kim Jones is a great talent and clearly good at refreshing existing material, but there's not necessarily a signature style, more of an attitude—which of course is what makes him so successful as a hired gun for luxury brands.

It's the same with Peter Copping, who has been at Oscar de la Renta, Nina Ricci, and Balenciaga. He's another brilliant designer, but I wouldn't point at something and say, "Very Peter Copping." Rick is an outlier in the era of LVMH and Kering. He carved out an aesthetic that appealed to the people who loved Rei Kawakubo and Helmut Lang, but it was all his own. And he literally owns it too. It's financially independent, so when you see Rick Owens, it's 100 percent Rick Owens and has specific codes. But for all those sculptural show pieces, the business has a bread and butter which is T-shirts, sweats, and boots. If he stopped selling those, the runway shows wouldn't happen.

KARLO: But those T-shirts don't have his logo blasted across the front of them. They still sell on the strength of design alone. The fabrication and cut seduce you. There is no other external signifier other than that it's his design.

MARK: Which is a stroke of genius. You get so few designers who have created a look that's so instantly identifiable without using branding. Even the label is discreet, each season detailed on a strip inside, but barely visible. I also love that he has expanded with brands that make sense. I wore Birkenstocks with Rick Owens before they created any collaborations. The combination makes perfect sense. It's stretching a point to call the sandals Brutalist, but there's a simplicity to them that fits with that aesthetic.

But then there are still designers who do, I believe, see their work as art and there is little scope of expanding it commercially. Carol Christian Poell, who you championed at Atelier, actively removed himself from the fashion calendar but still produces. His *Mainstream-Downstream* show in 2004 in Milan, with models floating down the river, was such a literal rejection of the way fashion is marketed. There hasn't been an official named collection since 2010, and only a few pieces continue to appear at random times in certain stores, but it's not a hype thing at all—his work is all about the discretion you mentioned earlier, and some of it is barely functional. You brought a suit by him to the studio for us to shoot from your archive, and the Self Edge reinforced red stitching is an incredible detail, invisible from outside [**pages 224–225**]. The construction is so stiff and narrow and extraordinary.

KARLO: He is unique. I want to make a statement here: I hope he never comes back. And I hope he never explains. Keep the legacy pure.

Of course, there will always be a market for things that are discreet, things defined by what is not seen. There will always be an alternative to the status quo, despite the all-seeing digital eye. There are people that are wearing felt costumes in basements right now, I guarantee it. It will always go on. But I do believe it is eroding, precisely because the culture absorbs things at a much faster rate than in the past and, once exposed, they wither and die. But that alternative will always exist. The bourgeoisie who will only ever shop at Hermès are the paramount.

MARK: Not everything you wear is by a major name. When you came to New York for us to shoot your archive, you were wearing a thrift store blazer five sizes bigger than your usual fit. What made you choose that on that day? Is it a case of having nothing to prove?

KARLO: I no longer expect fashion to save me. I am much more interested in style.

MARK: Subverting a tailor's intentions is certainly a style, and many of the designers associated with Atelier have played with proportions throughout their career. What do you see as the difference between tailoring and design? McQueen always said that everything he did was about tailoring, but he was also absolutely an avant-garde designer.

KARLO: Tailoring is about know-how. It is about technique and craft. Design? Not so much. Menswear is all about styling. If you want a beautifully tailored suit, you don't need a designer. It's there. It's been perfected. But if you want design, you go to a designer. Designers rarely bring anything new to the archetypes, they take away from them. Those archetypes have been perfected, which is why I am obsessed with uniforms. They are perfect for the task at hand. There are innovations in terms of technique and fabrication, but rarely does design add to the lexicon. Martin Margiela understood that perfectly, and that's why he did Replica. He would go to a vintage store, find a 1970s jacket with perfect proportions and pocket placement, and his ego allowed him to say, "This garment is perfect, there's nothing I can do to improve this." Some things don't need to be changed or improved on. Design offers you possibilities and exploration. It is a wonderful thing, but it's not tailoring.

MARK: Tailoring has been a default for men for generations, of course. Your influence has been in bringing those possibilities of new design to the fore as well as styling. Would you say there's a distinct DNA in your work as a stylist?

KARLO: Truthfully, I don't see a signature in my work, but others do. There are certain themes that reappear—androgyny is one of them. I like the idea of sex and sexuality to be beneath the surface. I prefer mystery and intrigue to something overt. Some of my heroes are Ray Petri from the 1980s, and Melanie Ward when she was working at the start of the 1990s. I like stylists who introduce elements that are no-go zones. With Ray it was bringing sportswear into tailoring and high fashion, with Melanie it was wearing trainers with everything. It was refreshing at the time. Both Panos Yiapanis and Samuel Drira influenced the look of Atelier more than any single designer. Today, I like Jo Barker and Ibrahim Kamara. Ib is a true image maker.

MARK: Ray Petri remains influential, and a lot of stylists have taken from his Buffalo aesthetic. He had a signature that you can't quite copy with authenticity. He was gay, and he put male models in skirts, but the styling was never camp. His men usually looked like boxers.

KARLO: I can see a yearning in his work. Like many gay men, he valued masculinity. But also, fundamentally, he was savvy and realized that putting a man in a skirt would be more digestible if it was presented in the way he styled it.

MARK: Petri used a lot of Gaultier in his shoots. The Gaultier show in Paris in 1985 was the first place we saw men in skirts, and a lot of the press walked out in protest, which seems quaint now.

KARLO: Despite what everyone thinks, fashion is a conservative business, and Paris at the time was particularly so. It was a highly binary time—men were men, women were women. Gender was hypersexualized: men were beefy and square jawed, women had wasp waists. It was easy to shock when that was the status quo.

MARK: And yet we have had kilts for centuries, and the skirts Gaultier designed in the 1980s had a proportion and cut to them that wasn't what you'd call feminine. They were a superb piece of contemporary design. In the 2020s the skirt for men is relatively common. Why was it shocking then and now almost mainstream?

KARLO: I think there was a shift in the early 1900s, when a certain kind of aristocratic opulence in menswear suddenly disappeared. I believe it was linked to the rise of America, and all that it symbolized. Men became more uniform in their appearance, and their dress was sombre and restrained. That aesthetic persevered for most of the twentieth century.

Perhaps the start of change was the hippie era when clothing became more unisex. Then there was the rise of nightclub culture in the 1970s. Suddenly there was a space that made all things permissible, and when you left that space, you had to walk home at 4 a.m. in whatever you were wearing. Other people caught glimpses of it and slowly everyone realized you could wear those clothes at 6 p.m. as well as midnight. Gaultier was an avid clubber and loved London, which is where his skirts came from, although they weren't really skirts—they had legs and a fold of fabric layered over them.

Fundamentally, the controversy of men in skirts has to do with the concept of masculinity, which is highly valued and treasured in Western culture. Masculinity is considered sacred and a driver of society, which is, of course, bullshit. It is okay for a woman to wear trousers because she is appropriating a valued attribute, but not so much when a man renounces masculinity. It takes a long time to chip away at that. Finally, today, we understand that a skirt is just a garment and has little to do with masculinity.

MARK: I am intrigued how other garments make a journey from radical to classic. A lot of Japanese designers you have worked with still incorporate a drop crotch in their trousers. It seemed a trend, but it's not gone away.

KARLO: I haven't personally worn drop crotch trousers since about 2010, but they still sell. The sensation of wearing them is similar to a skirt if you have a pair of balls—they leave space for your crotch just as skirts do. Sweatpants function in the same way. There's a physical liberation in that, which men find attractive. But drop crotch trousers aren't classic. A garment only becomes classic when it is beyond gender. Blue jeans and T-shirts are beyond gender. Boots are becoming beyond gender. Women aren't wearing drop crotch trousers, so they don't exist in that realm of the beyond. Because of that, they are subject to the eye becoming used to them, and therefore tired.

MARK: When I think of early Atelier, I think of racks and racks of black. Shapes may change, but black isn't going anywhere. Why? For me, personally, it's a fear of color because I don't know how to put it together, so black is a default. But what is it for you? Everything you brought to shoot from your archive was black.

KARLO: Black is powerful. It's impenetrable. It serves as a fortress. I have used clothing as a defence, and a way to declare that "I won." A lot of things I am attracted to tend to have black next to them. I love the look of the Black Panthers and their black leather. I love gothic horror. I love anything monastic or ecclesiastical, with long lines. I like black-and-white photography and early Japanese deconstruction—dark workwear. All these things resonate. Having said that, I do wear color. But you'll only see me in red if it's the inside of a cape and I am having a Count Dracula moment. I like military green and denim, gray and white.

MARK: All blacks are different. You can't just put one black garment with another, can you?

KARLO: The tonal qualities and textures are all different. There's a wide spectrum of blacks.

MARK: Who does it best?

KARLO: Yohji Yamamoto. I think he is more serious in his use of it than the other Japanese designers. I see Yohji as a poet—there is a deep sensitivity to the work. He loves women but he absolutely loves men too, and that is often overlooked. Even when his clothes are lavish or exaggerated, you get the impression that the person wearing those clothes probably won't let you down. And they may even have a knife in their pocket.

MARK: Black will always be with us, but there's been a highly visible movement towards color and graphics incorporated into a kind of folk vernacular in clothing, bordering on the naïve, or even outsider art. What's going on there?

KARLO: I anticipated this moment. We are at a time in history defined by cold artificiality—we have never been more connected, yet we've never been further apart. There is a deep sense of alienation, so we crave evidence of the human hand.

MARK: Clothes are absolutely about emotion. I'm interested in what you said about fashion as a form of defence. Sometimes clothing can be used as a means of assault, too—if you want to emphasize a certain queerness, for instance, you might wear a deliberately ugly thrift store floral dress and commando boots. Kurt Cobain pioneered the look at the start of the 1990s as a rejection of masculine and heteronormative dress codes, but it was also about distancing himself from a fashion world that had become obsessed with him. He set himself apart from the gendering of clothing, and the status quo and status of clothes generally, by wearing a $3 dress.

But fashion runs on the desire to invest in something that will give you confidence as much as it's about self-expression. You are a design-literate Black man who wears clothing that traditionally has been marketed to a wealthy white European customer. You have a successful career in fashion at a directorial level, so as you say, it's a declaration that you "won," but when most of the Black individuals in the industry are still models, fashion clearly has a problem. Where are the Black creative directors and members of the board? I remember when one of the Japanese designers launched their first collaboration with a sportswear brand. I went to the London flagship, and the shop assistant had just locked the door to prevent three Black men entering, on the pretense it was closing time. But it was mid-morning. After they walked away, she gestured for me to come back, to let me in. That was in the early 2000s, and I'm assuming it wouldn't happen today, but I'll never forget that moment.

KARLO: Try walking around any high-end department store or mono-brand boutique while being Black and see if you aren't followed. There have been some changes in fashion and in the wider culture, but they are mostly superficial. Fashion is like the Catholic church—it's a monolith that changes only after the world changes. Now fashion courts the hip-hop aristocracy, not because they necessarily want to, but because they have to or else they will look like they are stuck in a bygone era. When Black people display great talent or excellence, and I'm not saying that I do, it is often destabilizing to the white gaze. They don't know what to do with it. It causes them to reassess, which leads to discomfort.

I remember being with my partner Constantin von Haeften, who is white, and having several interactions with the CEO of an influential fashion house. Whenever he would speak with us, he would only address Constantin. He assumed that Constantin was the real power simply because he was white. That's just one example, but there have been many.

Coat by Maison Martin
Margiela (Artisanal),
Autumn/Winter 2000.

Coat by Yohji Yamamoto
Pour Homme,
Autumn/Winter 1999.

Shirt by Carpe Diem,
c. 2004.

Jacket by YSL (Atelier
signed exclusive),
Autumn/Winter 2010.

Hoodie by Raf Simons,
Spring/Summer 2003.

223

Suit by Carol Christian
Poell, Spring/Summer 2010.

Coat by Comme des
Garçons Homme Plus,
Autumn/Winter 1994.

Inverness cloak,
unsigned, Japanese,
c. 1940s.

11 | Karim Rashid

Cairo-born Canadian New Yorker Karim Rashid has designed over 4,000 products and won more than 300 awards, including the 2020 American Prize for Design, accorded by The Chicago Athenaeum: Museum of Architecture and Design and The European Centre for Architecture Art Design and Urban Studies. He holds honorary doctorates from OCAD University in Toronto, The Corcoran College of Art and Design in Washington, and Pratt Institute in Brooklyn. He has created hotels in Athens, Bergen, and Berlin, a sex shop in Munich, and a subway station in Naples, where he studied design under Ettore Sottsass, founder of Memphis.

Karim's brand is defined by curvilinear shapes, sheen, vibrant pop colors, and a refreshing optimism. Like his peers Philippe Starck and Marc Newson, he has remained focused on the idea of futurism, excited by the potential of technology that doesn't yet exist. His extraordinary client list includes 3M, Alessi, Artemide, Hugo Boss, Christofle, FontanaArte, Kenzo, Issey Miyake, Pepsi, Prada, Samsung, and Veuve Clicquot. He has designed over twenty-five realized hotels and fifty retail/restaurant spaces. Since the launch of his design studio in the early 1990s, Karim has embodied his design aesthetic, dressing entirely in white and super-bright colors, frequently incorporating his own graphics.

Karim Rashid in Hell's Kitchen, New York.
Suit by Hugo Boss; shirt by Dsquared2; shoes, Versus by Versace.

MARK: You are synonymous with color, but the rest of the world seems to be terrified of it unless it's on a pair of running shoes, or the beach. Pink is a signature for you. It's still seen as gendered in a reductive way, despite feminists trying their best to wrestle it away from the connotations it's been shackled with. And, of course, the pink triangle during the Holocaust was used to categorize and target gay men and transgender women. But pink has an inherently positive visual power. One of Diana Vreeland's most famous quotes came when she was talking to Norman Parkinson after he shot a fashion story in Jaipur for British *Vogue* in 1956: "How clever of you, Mr Parkinson, to know that pink is the navy blue of India."

KARIM: I love the idea of a singular monochromatic look, head to toe. If I'm wearing pink, the socks must be the same shade of pink as everything else. I have a drawer of underwear in every color to match my clothes. Even though you can't see it, I love the feeling of knowing it all goes together. I am obsessed with color. I first gravitated to pink when I was five years old. My mother took me to Selfridges in London, and we were looking for winter coats. I ran away from the boy's department, which was full of brown and blue, and towards a rack of pink coats. Children are naturally drawn to bright colors, and my mother was open-minded enough to let me wear what I wanted. Pink has a pure energy, it's such a positive color. Everybody responds to it in the same way. I had an eye exam three years ago and I was told I have four rather than three retinal cones, which is incredibly rare. It means I can see more colors. It's like RGB versus CMYK. It makes me wonder if that's where my intuitive feelings towards color come from.

MARK: Why are people afraid of color?

KARIM: Ninety-nine percent of our world is colorless today. I grew up in the 1960s, surrounded by color. There was the hippie movement, and tie-dye, and black light posters. It was in fashion but also interiors. Look at Stanley Kubrick's *A Clockwork Orange* (1972), which is maximalist from floor to ceiling. I remember in our little suburban house, we had a pink bathroom and a green refrigerator. Everyday objects used a lot of color.

I have a theory that as soon as we landed on the Moon in 1969, and realized that it was just a dead rock, we felt like we had nowhere to go. Until then, the future and everything space-age was so positive. It was the age of Isaac Asimov and Philip K. Dick. We were all going to live on other planets! Then, after all that optimism, we focused on Earth again. In the 1970s, the color palette for design was beige and brown. It was about trying to engage with nature. We had plants in our homes in a way we never did before. Then the brown slowly shifted to gray. And everything was monochromatic for a long time. I do think we are seeing something of a revival in color now, after the global pandemic.

MARK: Why do we default to black so often, particularly in fashion?

KARIM: Black is more interesting than many think. After the Beatniks of the 1950s and 1960s, it was only in the 1970s with the punk movement that black really started to happen in fashion. It grew out of London, and it wasn't commonly seen. I remember going to Rome when I was doing my master's degree when I was twenty-three—I had bright pink hair and wore all-black and was called a fascist. To wear black was controversial. It's totally accepted today, it's a badge of conformity. Ninety-five percent of kids at high school are wearing black with a black backpack.

We have all grown up with such an overwhelming pressure to conform. It starts in primary school, then you might have to wear a uniform for work. We have had 10,000 years of conforming for cultural, territorial, or religious reasons, when there's been a fear of the individual, but the digital age has changed that. We can all express and disseminate our ideas and we are all photographers and writers. There's a new respect for the idea of creativity, but at the same time, there's a paradox—everything starts to look the same.

I remember looking through a magazine of real estate on the plane home from Singapore a while back, and it was full of luxury condos that were identical. They all had off-white walls, a beige sofa, zero color. And if you looked at apartments in Milan, New York, or Cairo, they would have the same renderings. The digital age has given us the tools to disseminate trends to the point where the trend becomes overwhelming. So ultimately, we get conformity again.

MARK: I spoke to Philippe Starck recently about the future of design, and he believes that technology will free us from the physical object, and that when it comes to fashion and furniture, it will be conjured up through digital magic. We will all just be naked in an empty room, and we won't have traditional possessions or artifacts. What do you think will happen? Recycling denim and circularity can't, surely, be the last story we tell with fashion.

KARIM: I think eventually we'll drop physical clothing. We will develop a surface that gets sprayed on our body, a liquid crystal polymer will be attached to your skin, and it will make sure that you never feel hot or cold, according to the way it reacts to ambient temperature. You will be able to fire up imagery on the surface, change the color at will, and have video or words on it.

Analog clothing is done. Everything is made from the same blocks, and fashion is all about manipulating those same blocks. You can't do anything original with it, as it stands, but it's a huge economic machine—so no matter what brand you are, you make the same five-pocket jeans. When Levi's created that design in the late 1800s, it was for a function. We don't live that way now. Fashion has a desperation to do something new, but all it does is perpetually look at the past. We might be in what will be called the age of casualism, or data-driven design right now. We won't know what it is until it ends. And then people will look back on that too.

A lot of fashion education is about looking at past trends rather than other design mediums, so it's a dead end. It's not design, it's styling. It's inspired by human behavior from the past. Cufflinks and ties are irrelevant. The shirt collar is redundant. A lot of fashion remains theater. It's costume. What you wear to a cocktail party—that's not clothing to me. Clothing should be about function as well as expression. We should be looking at performance fabrics. I like jewelry, but it has no function, so it should bring more to us today, because it can. I wear a ring by Oura which monitors biometric data twenty-four hours a day and gives me stats on my sleep cycle, REM, and temperature. There's so much potential with everything we put on our body.

MARK: You've worked on clothing design before. We photographed the Cybercouture jacket you designed with Pia Myrvold in 2000, in white with reflective line detailing [**page 246**]. It looks futuristic, but I wonder how you feel it has dated?

KARIM: That jacket was ahead of its time. The pockets were all designed for function—the upper pocket was perfect for the iPhone that would appear seven years later, and there was a pocket for your laptop charger. No one had really created garments with technology in mind at that point. The same year I designed it, I worked on the single-dose packaging for Prada Skincare. I also designed bags and purses for them, which were all super-high-tech, but none of it made it into production. Even now when I design bags, I'm forced to do conventional copies of what we consider an archetype of a handbag.

MARK: I remember how exciting the Prada Skincare packaging was when it came out. I bought a lot of it. It felt totally new, and it now also seems prescient—the way you unwrapped each capsule was so clinical and sterile, not unlike a Covid test. It's interesting that you say fashion is so resistant to technology. Do you think there's an obvious way forward?

KARIM: Everybody is copying each other. People like Yohji Yamamoto and Issey Miyake made a huge impact because they did something that no one had done before, and they stuck to it. Most of fashion now has no sense of identity. There's no vision. A lot of brands just put their name on something to differentiate it from an identical product. That's not design.

MARK: It might be the case that technology will change fashion in the way that digital mediums have changed everything else, but we can't comprehend it quite yet. The MP3, the camera phone, and cashless retail have changed our lives in radical ways. Digital printing is something that's only just starting to achieve its potential, and at some point the price point of it will shift from Iris van Herpen couture to mass-market accessibility.

Karim Rashid in Hell's Kitchen, New York.
Suit custom-made by My Suit, *c.* mid-2010s;
T-shirt by Keith Haring/Uniqlo, 2016;
sneakers by Reebok x Opening Ceremony, 2016.

But I wonder if the future of fashion will be shaped more by engineering than pattern cutting—which also makes me think about how your aesthetic was honed. You studied with Ettore Sottsass and Gaetano Pesce in Italy. Ettore gave us the color palette for postmodernism with Memphis, and Gaetano is still as radical as ever. I spent an afternoon at his studio a few years ago, and he's so candid and refreshing. He was telling me how he felt American design had its moment with the Shakers and Charles and Ray Eames, and then it all went wrong. He buys a new Norma Kamali Sleeping Bag Coat every season, in a different color, because he loves the concept of it, but he cited Michael Kors as a "disaster" and expressed despair that he was the biggest fashion designer in America. I have a lot of respect for Michael Kors, and think he's done some amazing work, but for a long time the MK logo was rinsed out via merchandising and fakes, and I understand what he means. Gaetano's credo is that you must divorce art and experimentation from money for it to work. What did you learn from Sottsass and Pesce?

KARIM: I learned a lot about color. When I was studying in Canada, we weren't allowed to put any color in the models for our projects. For four years, everything I did was black, white, or gray. One of the reasons I wanted to study with Sottsass was that he mixed colors that you'd never think about putting together, and always with the right shape and balance of composition. I went to the opening of Memphis in 1983, which happened to be my birthday, and I remember looking at the pieces and the sensibility, and it made me want to express what had been dormant in me.

But of course when I went back to Canada and I wanted to work with color, it wasn't that easy. One of my first jobs was to create a laptop for Toshiba. It was eleven kilos, huge. I showed them renderings using baby blue and a light pink, and they freaked out. All the computers until that point were an ugly beige, like they were made of plastic that had faded in the sun. I have no idea why that had become the norm. I persuaded them to go with a cool gray, so at least I had made some difference.

After that I tried repeatedly to introduce color into products, but no one wanted to use it. In 1993, when I founded my own studio, I had a meeting with Umbra and showed them 400 tints of PPE polymer. We started working on a range of incredible products using color, as well as injection metallics. I used techniques that Gaetano had showed me to mix colors together. We launched the Garbo and Oh chairs, but, significantly, the colors didn't stay on the market. About six million Oh chairs have been sold, but today they just make them in black or white.

MARK: You have elevated graphics, as well as slogans, within your work. You've incorporated your own image into a lot of those graphics, which is great marketing. What makes a good graphic?

KARIM: I love abstraction and minimalism. If I use a graphic, it should be strong and minimal. Keith Haring did it so well. Warhol too. I called my work "digipop" for a long time because I saw it as following in the tradition of 1960s pop art, but using techniques they didn't have back then. If I create a crazy wireframe, that's what Victor Vasarely was doing back in the 1930s, but what I can do now, he could never have done by hand.

MARK: You've also explored the use of slogans on objects, particularly clothing, which I'm interested in. It goes back to when Malcolm McLaren and Vivienne Westwood were workshopping punk in the 1970s, and it's remained a tool for high impact: in 2020 Willie Norris created a range of T-shirts with "PROMOTE HOMOSEXUALITY" on them. That's a simple agitprop statement, a slogan that could be reproduced without buying the original, but there's a sense of being part of a group, and the power in belonging to that group, by sourcing it from Norris, who is a trans designer. It's a signifier, for those who recognize it.

Slogans are such a powerful way to transform a simple garment. One of Martin Margiela's most famous designs is his simplest—the T-shirt he created in 1994 for the charity AIDES with the text "THERE IS MORE ACTION TO BE DONE TO FIGHT AIDS THAN WEAR THIS T-SHIRT BUT IT'S A GOOD START" on it. He had it silkscreened on the garment while it's folded, so when worn you need to study it, and the wearer, to decipher the whole text. Which is the point. It's about creating a conversation. Other designers use text in a more straightforward and rhetorical way, rather like shouting at you. Katharine Hamnett was the queen of the medium in the 1980s. The first T-shirt she made was "CHOOSE LIFE" in 1981, inspired by her interest in Buddhism. Then she created a series of anti-nuclear messages, and in 1984 the photograph of her wearing her "58% DON'T WANT PERSHING" as she shook hands with Margaret Thatcher at Downing Street became worldwide news. It's similar to memes we see today where an image of a celebrity holding a blank surface is Photoshopped to carry a witty phrase or polemic, but Hamnett did it in real life. She turned up with her jacket buttoned up, then revealed the slogan just as she was about to meet Thatcher. Like "SILENCE = DEATH," "THANK GOD FOR ABORTION," or "MAKE AMERICA GREAT AGAIN," it showed how powerful and disruptive a slogan can be, in the right context.

KARIM: I think Hamnett is a great example of that. Absolutely wonderful. So is the artwork that Barbara Kruger produces. I think the whole world has modernized and looks a certain way now. You can see it in food packaging, which is now more minimal. It's about the beauty of a simple message. There's too much visual information out there, so something simple and strong stands out. The packaging I created for Method in the early 2000s was minimalist, and no one was doing that for the supermarket shelves. Now it's common. We have so much distraction.

The slogan T-shirt I created in 2001, with "I AM NOT A TERRORIST" in bright pink text on the back, came about because I was being constantly stopped at airports in New York when I flew back to the States [page 239]. I had a Canadian passport with my place of birth recorded as Cairo. I spent hours in little rooms in Newark, LaGuardia, and JFK, being interrogated because of my name and where I was born. I wore that T-shirt proudly whenever I flew, and it was done deliberately to provoke.

MARK: Provocation is something fashion still has the power to do.

KARIM: Absolutely. But it can be in lots of different forms. It's obvious I like attention. I remember I was flying Business class for the first time, from London to New York in 1996, and there was a guy sitting near me, staring at me. He was middle-aged, and dressed in a suit, while I was wearing head to toe pastel pink. He was staring at me for so long that I was going to ask him to stop, but just as I was about to, he said: "You look amazing. I love what you're wearing." And that felt great. I thought, wow, here's the most conservative-looking person I can imagine, giving me a compliment. And it made me realize I needed to keep doing what I was doing.

Often someone says, "You can really pull that off," and what does that really mean? It means they admire you, but they're too afraid to try it themselves. So you keep doing it, and it's a small provocation, and you start to make change. Wearing color can make people a little bit more open-minded about everything.

Leather coat by Versace, 1995; sweater and beanie by ASOS, 2021.

Custom-made suit
by Versace, 2018.

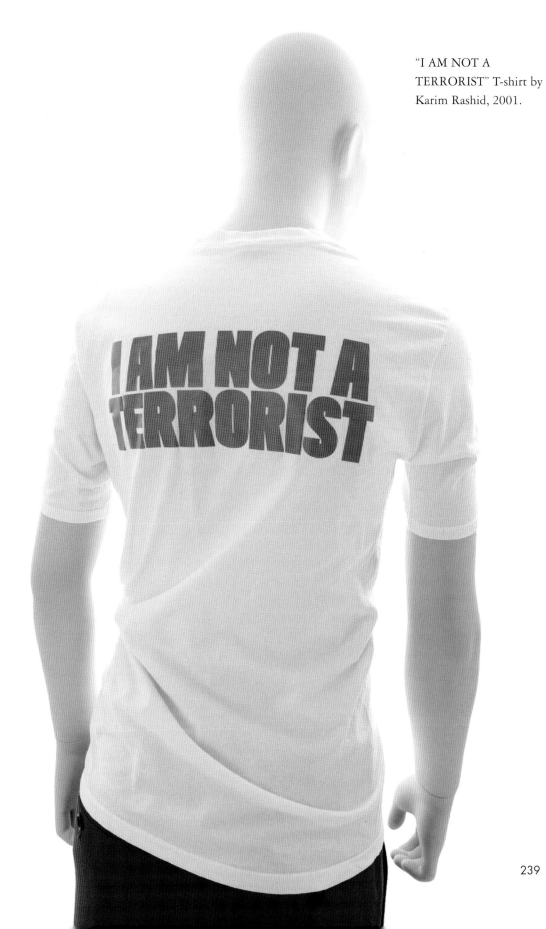

"I AM NOT A TERRORIST" T-shirt by Karim Rashid, 2001.

239

White raincoat by
Hugo Boss, 2020.

Fabric and suit using
laminate pattern
created by Abet
Laminati for Kasa
Karim collection, 2010.

241

White coat by
Rad Hourani, 2013.

Raincoat by Stutterheim x
Henrik Vibskov, 2017.

Hoodie by Dsquared2, 2013;
jeans by Marc Jacobs, 2012;
jacket by Helmut Lang, 2017.

244

Black jacket by Nicol
Lebedinskaya (design student
based in Odessa), 2021.

245

Jacket by Cybercouture,
designed by Karim Rashid
and Pia Myrvold, 2000.

Karimoji T-shirt by
Karim Rashid, 2014.

247

12 | Steven Philip

Steven Philip's collection consists of past moments from British fashion that couldn't happen today. His clothes embody the analog DIY attitude of a time when communication took place in nightclubs and research was carried out in libraries and museums, not online. His encyclopedic knowledge and obsessive interest in the work of largely London-based designers from the 1980s is second to none, and his archive has become an indispensable resource for stylists and designers looking for something authentic to throw into their mix. Alongside early John Galliano and BodyMap, he owns rare, esoteric leather pieces by Issey Miyake, hallucinatory floaty florals by Zandra Rhodes from the 1970s, body-con Alaïa, and the streetstyle-goes-to-the-first-arrondissement work of Jean Paul Gaultier from the 1980s.

Scottish-born Steven left Dundee for London full time in 1987 to collaborate with his close friend, the late singer Billy Mackenzie. He had already been visiting the capital for years, immersing himself in what was one of the most exciting movements in fashion of all time. Steven began to buy regularly from the most influential boutiques, including Worlds End, Bazaar, and Jones, and acquired numerous privately commissioned pieces from Leigh Bowery. Slowly he began to build a business, trading select pieces with friends, and then selling them on Portobello Road Market. Before setting up the Steven Philip Studio in Brighton, he was co-founder of the vintage store Rellik. Today, he works as a consultant for fashion historians, curators, and design houses, and continues to add to his personal collection.

Steven Philip at the V&A, London.
Jacket by Kim Jones for Louis Vuitton, print by the Chapman Brothers.

MARK: We've vaguely known each other for years through London clubs, but I remember the first time we met professionally was when I was in touch with you about a John Flett coat in black cashmere with white buttons that I was thinking about selling. I'd bought it around 1987 from Bazaar on South Molton Street. Flett was so important in fashion—he was Galliano's partner for a while—but died so young, at twenty-seven, at the start of the 1990s. I cherished that coat. I had such good times in it. We talked about that, then we talked about what things interested you generally, and I remember telling you I also had an Anna Sui shearling coat that I'd spent a fortune on in New York in the late 1990s and was thinking about selling that too. You told me it wasn't something for you because there was no resonance or story, it was "product," and I should just gift it to a friend who would enjoy it, which I did. When do you think fashion became product rather than design?

STEVEN: I think after 1989. That's when people started to want to remortgage their house just to buy something that was luxury. Product for me is when something has to be sold to you, and design is something that you look at and say, "Oh my god, I love the creators behind this, I love the look and effect of it—this is art." You never had product when things were based in street culture because you couldn't market it, although many people did try. When you get punk trousers from H&M, that's the epitome of product.

MARK: But then I think about someone like Gaultier, whose whole aesthetic in the 1980s was forged by coming to London and channeling streetstyle into something luxurious. He represented rebellion, but he also made those exquisite shirts and suits for Gibo.

STEVEN: A very good point and example. In the 1980s you'd go to Kings Cross Station, get into the photobooth with your friend, then pin the photos on your jacket and go dancing at The Bell. Gaultier took that idea and created little frames with "Jean Paul Gaultier" on them. That was so clever, and in a way, yes, it was about creating product—but it wasn't cynical.

MARK: Sometimes a label totally changes direction. I keep thinking about the McQueen narrative, and how Lee went from being an iconoclast to creating pure product. He was so hungry to create a brand. When he was given the Givenchy backing, it stopped being about his club kid friends and became all about the business of luxury. It was so shocking in a way when the first fragrance and body products with his name on came out—it felt like five minutes earlier he had just been our mate spilling beer over his boyfriend at Beautiful Bend at Central Station. The priorities seemed a world apart.

STEVEN: Whether you like it or not, we are part of a generation that is forced to do that now. No matter what kind of designer you think you are, you have to create product. It's the same with anything creative. Do you think fine artists really want to do limited edition prints? When

Peter Blake, the greatest artist on Earth, does a limited edition of 150, it is product. Very few people can stay out of that arena. Even Vivienne Westwood moved into it. It became part of what defined her brand.

MARK: As with McQueen as a brand, I find it so strange to go into TK Maxx and see racks of Westwood in there, with the orb emblems on the breast pocket. For so many of us her name and label were so underground and authentic and had such an insider kind of resonance.

STEVEN: It's quite sad, but then, who isn't in TK Maxx now, apart from Hermès and Chanel? The reason I'm still so enthusiastic about Vivienne and Malcolm McLaren is because of the story attached to those early pieces—as with Gaultier, it's about a narrative. When I look at John Galliano, he was part of a crowd of people that we all admired, including John Flett, John Crancher, and Judy Blame. Absolutely none of that was about product. They didn't know how to market or sell anything, and they didn't care. Leigh Bowery absolutely didn't want to sell clothes. It was all about creating stuff for your friends to wear, not shifting 20,000 units of something.

MARK: So are we saying that commerciality is fatal for any kind of creativity? Can the two be balanced at all?

STEVEN: Galliano went bankrupt several times. It was a bumpy road for him. For most of his early career he was doing it all on a shoestring, driven by passion. When he went to Dior, all he had to do was play the game—but he never played the total game with the designs. With Dior Couture, it was all illusion and fantasy. You'd never be able to buy into it, so instead the Dior brand would sell tens of thousands of products like bags, beauty, and ready to wear. But you could never buy into the true talent and illusion of John.

MARK: Like you, I'm fixated by John Galliano's early work. He was doing the most revolutionary cutting and styling and the way he presented it in such a holistic way, with Amanda Harlech styling and Jeremy Healy playing records, was incredible.

STEVEN: For me it is about the thought that went into the work—he had, and has, such knowledge about how to shape and work with fabric. I don't know where some of those early silhouettes came from. I have lots of it, including work from his first ever show in 1984 [**pages 260–261**]. The shapes and fabrics are truly incredible and still look radical.

MARK: One of the other most compelling things about Galliano was always the story behind each collection, which might incorporate Tennessee Williams, Cleopatra, or Pocahontas.

STEVEN: Yes, and I feel like those kinds of narratives don't necessarily exist anymore. Narrative is not that important—or it certainly doesn't sit at the core of a collection. Today if there's a story behind a collection, it's a short story. I don't want a short story—I want an epic! When Galliano showed that first collection, *Les Incroyables*, he was telling a whole story about the French revolution in both history and attitude. The detail was incredible, with smashed magnifying glasses worn as jewelry, and rainbow-colored ribbons sewn on the insides of coats [**pages 260–261**].

There's a misconception today, I think, about those designers who were so influential from 1979 to 1989—Galliano, Stevie Stewart and David Holah of BodyMap, and many of their peers. People think it was just a bunch of kooky club kids who were all on drugs and running bits of fabric through an overlocker, but they actually had an intensely intellectual approach. They were meticulous about research. It wasn't like today where everything's on an iPhone. You'd go to a museum, you'd read a book, you'd look at pattern techniques. I really believe—and not just because I'm old and I don't like social media—that all of that has been taken away from us.

MARK: When did your personal collection start? Did you know you were actually collecting when it began?

STEVEN: Fashion became a business for me around twenty-five years ago. I'd been traveling with Billy Mackenzie in America and then I settled in Berlin for six months. I loved being there. I was in the city when the wall came down. For this little boy from Dundee, those experiences were hugely exciting for me.

When I got home, I started to think about what I really wanted to do with my life. My friend had a stall on Portobello Road, and I thought to myself: "I could do something here." It was the early 1990s, and Oxford Street—all of London, really—was a sea of gray and black. We'd gone minimal with Calvin Klein and Prada. I was thinking, "Where's the color? Where are the Vivienne Westwood *Harris Tweed* crowns? Where is the new John Galliano? Where is the fire?" There was something really missing. Thank God Alaïa and Helmut Lang saved the day with their futuristic vision. But I also had a craving to bring back the fun from the early part of the 1980s, to reintroduce some of the vibe that we had at Kensington Market and Hyper Hyper. So I set up a stall selling vintage, and word spread. I used to buy 1970s floral shirts and get images of Marc Bolan and David Bowie printed on them. I sold old Vivienne Westwood that I bought from people who had grown up, had kids, and didn't wear it anymore. As with a lot of things in life, it all just fell into place. And I started keeping specific pieces for myself. Like, if you own a vintage car lot, you might keep the best cars, and you might sell a Rolls Royce to buy a car that Elvis owned. Or like the secondary art market, where you sell stuff to buy new pieces.

I really believe that collectability is about a collective memory. The other day I saw a photograph of Holly Johnson wearing a Vivienne Westwood leather armor jacket from her *Time*

Machine collection in 1988 and a John Bull hat, and it has such resonance. That leather jacket is very rare, and I love it.

MARK: So would you say the collection began by accident?

STEVEN: With the Westwood pieces, it wasn't an accident, it was a hobby. It was like building a jigsaw. I had so many pieces, but I always wanted to complete a look—the coat, the waistcoat, the trousers, and the squiggle-print *Pirate* shirt [**pages 268–269**]. I realized there was more financial gain in that as well, because I was creating museum-quality ensembles. If it's just one jacket, people go, "Oh, that's great," but if it's the whole look, then they get really excited— "Oh my god, that should be in a museum!" I was very fortunate, because I was one of the first people to be looking at and appreciating all the old Westwood.

MARK: How did you source all those pieces? Where did you look?

STEVEN: Because this was before Instagram and before smartphones, people actually spoke to one another. I would have conversations on the stall on Portobello Road. I'd say that eight out of ten people in the world of clubs and fashion had sold me a piece at a certain point, bringing me a Richard Torry cardigan or a Galliano jacket to make some money. Word went out that I would buy things at a fair price, then maybe sell it to someone else I knew was interested. I've worked a lot with Kim Jones over the past ten years, helping him to build his archive. He's got the most amazing collection ever.

MARK: Kim has a celebrated collection of 1980s pieces from Worlds End and the House of Beauty and Culture. I wondered if you might actually be competition for him, fighting over the same pieces.

STEVEN: We actually don't overlap too much—he's not really into Galliano, for instance, which is my thing. But he does collect early Westwood and McLaren, as do I. We have been friends for years, so it's a bit like swapping football cards: I find pieces for him, and he keeps an eye out for pieces he knows I am missing. We work together.

MARK: You worked with Malcolm McLaren, didn't you?

STEVEN: Yes, he was working on an installation in 1999 in Maastricht, as part of an exhibition at the Bonnefanten Museum called *Smaak* (On Taste), and he borrowed eighteen pieces from me. He came up to my tiny studio, and all the stuff I had was in bin liners, crammed in a cupboard. I got it out and threw it all over the floor. None of it had been washed or anything. You should have seen the state of some of the pieces—they'd been worn at shooting galleries. But Malcolm was thrilled. He said: "It's so exciting to see it all like this—this is how it should be displayed. It was never meant to be stored in acid-free tissue." He loved it. I have kept a few full punk ensembles, but it's difficult to collect now. The bubble burst because of the commercialism and fakes. It was becoming too much like hard work to maintain a collection.

MARK: You're quite negative about social media but you do use Instagram and have a huge following on there—almost everyone I know in fashion follows you. I love it when you post new pieces from your collection, and as with what you said about those vintage Westwood and McLaren pieces, I love how casual it is—it's often just thrown on the floor. It looks great. It has a wonderful energy to it.

STEVEN: That's me trying to pass something on to the youth. I always have time for students. When they come in the studio, I often talk about Judy Blame—I show them some of his stuff and say, "Look, if you can't make something amazing out of just a ball of wool, you can't do what you're trying to do." You don't need the best fabric; you just need to make your vision work. I knew all those kids were on Instagram, watching, so every Saturday morning I started doing pictures from the collection with a description. If those kids are going to look at their fucking phone all day, they may as well get educated rather than look at another H&M advert.

MARK: You collect both menswear and womenswear. Is it harder to get good menswear? The auction houses seem to focus mostly on womenswear.

STEVEN: It is much harder. I think men have a different relationship with their clothes. Men tend to keep things. They don't seem to move things on. If a man got a shirt from Gaultier in 1998, it may not fit him anymore, but he'll still remember paying £350 for it, so he won't part with it. I think a lot of the really good stuff is stuck in someone's wardrobe somewhere, but I think we will start to see more of it appear when people realize there's a market for it.

I don't want to generalize, but women tend to move on. They like change. In the 1980s, when a girl put together an outfit she was already thinking about the next outfit. She needed her next hit. Men just kept going in the same outfit a year or so, and still wanted to keep it. They wore their clothes into oblivion. You'd wear your Rachel Auburn jumper and your *Pirate* trousers every day. Some of the Westwood stuff I have seen has been in a terrible state, but I still come across great pieces. And I sold a lot of menswear pieces that I would call diamonds. I miss them. There was a Westwood and McLaren Buffalo jacket with embellishment on the lapels, and I had the best one money could buy, which I got from Pete Burns. I sold that to Japan. That was a wonderful piece.

MARK: I want to talk about BodyMap, which was the label that had the most resonance for me growing up in London. It was what Michael Clark was wearing, and everyone at Taboo and The Bell. If you wore something by David Holah and Stevie Stewart with a Hilde Smith print on, it marked you at as being an insider in certain circles. I remember looking at a sweater in a store in Kensington and just being so desperate to have it. I took it off the hanger, but I was too intimidated to even try it on—it was everything to me, but I couldn't afford it. What do you think made BodyMap so special?

STEVEN: They ticked a giant box by bringing the whole sportswear element to fashion before anyone else. It was before Adidas and Nike had any kind of fashion appeal. And their clothes were very easy to move in—they were great to dance in, so they had club appeal. It was also easy to manufacture, and the shapes had a good way of conveying a print. Suddenly there was a whole movement around that style, with Rachel Auburn and Pam Hogg and others working in similar fabrics and focusing on prints.

MARK: BodyMap had such a distinct vocabulary, and of course David and Stevie were a huge success almost straight from college, but cash flow and the logistics of actually running a fashion business killed the label. It's been so hard to launch a label in London ever since, unless you have massive backing. It's virtually impossible to make money, even when everyone is working in the studio for next to nothing. McQueen did it and made a success of it, but do you think he will be seen as the last to manage that?

STEVEN: He was maybe the last emperor. But then I see Charles Jeffrey and his team doing something really interesting. As you say, it's all about survival. To be creative, you have to be in an environment where you don't give a fuck about anything, but the kids today have to give a fuck. A cup of tea and a sandwich is twenty quid in London now. I think these days, more of the youth have to work together as a little team. And this will make them stronger, rather than an individual chasing the star system. But Charles has excitement at his shows, and he tells a story. He has a lot of young kids involved in telling that story, and it's great, although I think it's diluted by social media. I think back to how thrilling it was to go to Alexander McQueen's *It's a Jungle Out There* show in 1997—the energy was amazing, and that's something you cannot communicate through social media. Everything is streamed live now, but years ago it took months before things were articulated in the media, and it was all done more artfully. Today a designer might work for weeks on a pocket detail, and it's on a screen for a second. I loved it when Tom Ford banned photographers at his shows. You can't watch theater on TV. It doesn't work.

MARK: As well as BodyMap, which particularly significant designers from the 1979–89 period have now slipped off the cultural radar, do you think?

STEVEN: John Flett didn't really slip off the radar, he just died too young. He had such a beautiful, beautiful, beautiful cut. Amazing. He definitely inspired John Galliano. John Crancher, too, who died in 1993. Also, Rifat Ozbek, though again he didn't fall off the radar, he just decided to leave the fashion arena.

I'm still amazed by Christopher Nemeth and his collection made out of postal sacks. I think what they're doing with the Nemeth label now is good, but I don't think you can recreate the *Mona Lisa*. Something like that only works if it is limited, and not for the masses. How do you recreate Judy Blame? Is someone going to take that name on and create things as a brand? You couldn't do it. You also have to move on. I do live a lot in the past, but that's about what was significant to me. I've also got to think of the future, and I want these kids to define something new. It was like in the 1970s, you couldn't just keep listening to the Beatles for the whole decade.

MARK: We photographed an early Chris Nemeth piece from your collection, and I was intrigued by the story behind it [**page 263**]. I was in touch with his widow Keiko in Tokyo, and she remembers that Chris was wearing a near-identical jacket the day she first met him, at a Galliano show in London. The back panel was made from a rug that had been on the floor of his studio. The uniqueness and memories attached to that garment are significant. It tells a story about London in a certain era, and London seems to be a common link to a lot of your archive.

But at the same time Nemeth and BodyMap were visible in clubs in London, Stephen Sprouse was happening in New York. His approach was similar to what was going on in London. I see him as the answer to Vivienne Westwood, in a way, because so much of it was counterculture plugged into music. Do you think he was an anomaly in America?

STEVEN: I am hugely interested in Stephen Sprouse. We were all brought up with Debbie Harry and she only wore Sprouse. She is in our blood. One of the most exciting things to happen in fashion in recent years was Marc Jacobs using Sprouse's imagery for Louis Vuitton. The contrast was amazing because Louis Vuitton is pure Hollywood. That luggage is the stuff that dreams are made of—you need to work for a year to afford a piece of it. So to see Sprouse—who is from the street and known for day-glo pop and PVC boots—all over those trunks is amazing. To think that women in Beverly Hills were walking around with Stephen Sprouse graffiti on their bags made me smile. They wouldn't have looked twice at his work and the world he represented when he was alive, but now they love it.

MARK: One of the things I really enjoyed after Marc Jacobs used the Sprouse graphics was seeing all the fakes everywhere. Seeing his name written on bags sold on markets everywhere from Brixton to Bangkok is quite brilliant. As you say, he was so underground and so niche, and now he's dead he's a kind of global brand.

STEVEN: I couldn't agree with you more. If Stephen Sprouse hadn't passed away, he would have died laughing.

Shirt, waistcoat, and jacket by John Galliano, *Afghanistan Repudiates Western Ideals* collection, Spring/ Summer 1985.

Waistcoat by John Galliano,
Les Incroyables collection,
graduation show, June 1984.

Suit by John Galliano,
The Ludic Game collection,
Autumn/Winter 1985.

Jacket by Chris
Nemeth, 1986.

263

Red velvet ensemble by
Pam Hogg, *Warrior Queen*
collection, 1988.

264

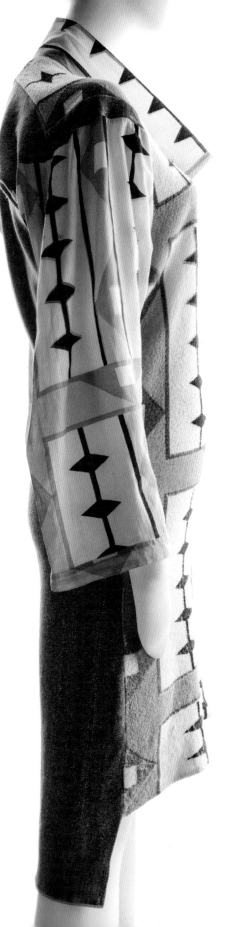

Shirt/dress by Worlds End (Malcolm McLaren and Vivienne Westwood), *Savage* collection, Spring/Summer 1982.

Four-piece ensemble suit by
Vivienne Westwood, *Anglomania*
collection, Autumn/Winter 1993.

266

Jacket by Leigh Bowery, c. 1986.

267

Head-to-toe ensemble
by Worlds End
(Malcolm McLaren and
Vivienne Westwood),
Pirate collection,
Autumn/Winter 1981.

269

Catsuit by Rifat Ozbek,
Autumn/Winter 1989.

270

Bolero jacket, bra, and trousers
by Rifat Ozbek, 1988.

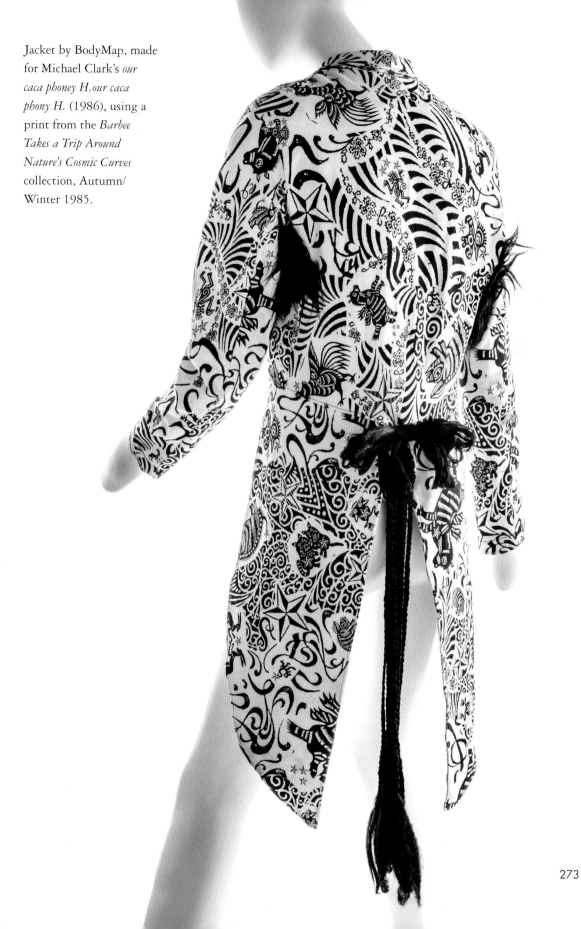

Jacket by BodyMap, made for Michael Clark's *our caca phoney H.our caca phony H.* (1986), using a print from the *Barbee Takes a Trip Around Nature's Cosmic Curves* collection, Autumn/Winter 1985.

273

13 | Desmond is Amazing

Desmond Napoles is best known as Desmond is Amazing. Born in 2007, they started going with their parents to the Pride March in New York City as a toddler and took part in the parade for the first time at the age of eight. After being filmed vogueing along Sixth Avenue in a rainbow-colored tulle skirt and matching gold sequin vest and bonnet, Desmond became a viral sensation: the image of a child on the streets of Manhattan enjoying and celebrating the freedoms fought for by the pioneers of Stonewall captured the imagination of many, while inspiring predictable fury from a reactionary fringe. "Haters," as Taylor Swift once sang, "gonna hate."

Since then, Desmond has modeled at New York Fashion Week, acted in the Gia Coppola film *Mainstream* (2020), cut the ribbon at the 2017 NYC DragCon alongside RuPaul, and launched the Haus of Amazing and Haus of Amazing Junior—online communities for LGBTQ+ and gender diverse youth, teens, and their allies—as well as the Haus of Darlings, a supportive group for parents, guardians, educators, and supporters of LGBTQ+ gender non-conforming youth. In 2020 they published *Be Amazing: A History of Pride*, aimed at readers aged three to nine, and in 2021 Desmond is Amazing released their debut single "We Are Amazing." In 2022 they launched a clothing line, Be Amazing NYC, followed by a range of sneakers in 2023.

Desmond lives with their parents Wendy and Andrew Napoles in New York. Wendy works closely with Desmond on all their creative projects as manager, collaborator, and guardian, and was a part of our conversation.

Desmond is Amazing in the East Village, New York.
Suit by OppoSuits, shirt by Target.

MARK: This is the second time we have met for this book. The first time, I shot you on the street in Bushwick, in the summer of 2019 [**page 279**]. We had lunch in a café that's now gone, along with a lot of things in the city. This project was on hold because of the global pandemic. You are now almost unrecognizable from how you looked back then, so we're shooting again. You've grown into a teenager, but also now you're wearing suits rather than dresses. What prompted that shift?

DESMOND: Everything I did used to be about big costumes and full-on drag. I still enjoy doing that, but during the pandemic I was home-schooling and not doing much else, so I used that time to experiment and see what fit with how I was feeling. I developed a new style. I still have all that other stuff in me, just not as much as I used to. After not doing drag for about three or four months, I started looking at a combination of boy's clothes and makeup, and that felt more like me.

I still love dresses, particularly ones that stop just above the knee, and I like gowns and formal and couture dresses too. But now it's a variety. I am really into my suits in bright red or blue.

MARK: A lot of designers aren't gendering their clothes now. You say you started wearing boy's clothes, and you're wearing a button-down shirt. What makes something gendered for you?

DESMOND: It's just clothes, really. Ultimately, it's not gendered. Whatever I wear is whatever I wear.

MARK: You now have a significant archive of costumes. Some of them are vintage gowns, some are custom-made. Tell me about how some of those costumes have come into existence. Where do the ideas come from?

DESMOND: I have two couture gowns by designer Malan Breton. I first met Malan around 2017 when he invited me to his movie screening and show at Fashion Week. That's also the time I met an amazing model named Rain Dove. I have gone to all of Malan's New York shows since then—he is a big inspiration to me. I've always kept in touch with Malan on social media and he gifted me two gowns [**pages 283 and 285**].

Another designer I'm close friends with is Richie Rich. He's a huge inspiration to me, and I love his positive attitude and style. All that glitter! I see a lot of myself in Richie. The first time I met him, we had on the exact same heart-shaped sunglasses. I really admired his gender-bending style when he was a club kid, and his fashion line Heatherette. He handmade me my sweater dress, with its heart pattern of large sequins [**page 288**]. I modeled for him at the start of 2023. He launched his new label Richerette. The show started with the Fleetwood Mac song 'Go Your Own Way'. I wore mismatched sneakers, a bronze pleated skirt and a T-shirt with "CLUB KID FAN CLUB" on the front.

There is also a custom jacket I received from a brand called The Series [**pages 290–291**]. They messaged me and said they would love to make me something. When I saw it for the first time, I was shocked. They had taken some of my mottos and hand-sewn them on to the jacket. I love that they upcycled fabric and materials for it. Sustainability is a big issue, and the fashion industry is so wasteful. I recommend a movie called *The True Cost* (2015) to learn more about that.

I also have a custom-made unicorn costume by a brand called Coquetry Clothing [**page 289**]. I wore it for my music video for "We Are Amazing." I wanted something to send a message to kids that are getting bullied. I wanted them to realize that they are a thousand times more amazing than the people who bully them.

MARK: You've adopted a few celebrity personas to perform in over the years. You did a Kurt Cobain look which was interesting—Cobain said he loved a "cosy flower pattern," and he used to play with gender fluidity. He was a vocal feminist and defender of gay rights. In the 2020s, a lot of queer boys and gender-fluid individuals have adopted his look. How did you become aware of him?

DESMOND: I knew a lot about him because my mom grew up listening to that music. I showed my mom a photo I liked of him and she helped me get the things I needed from eBay and thrift stores to recreate the look. When I first heard the song "Smells Like Teen Spirit" I was like, "Wow!" Then I listened to *Nevermind* (1991). It sounds so different from the music we have today. My mom told me about how Cobain was a voice for her generation, and how sad she was when he died. She also showed me a lot of photos of him in dresses. He didn't try to look like a woman—he was just a man in a dress. I relate to that because I like to mix masculine outfits with something feminine. I also love that Kurt Cobain covered the David Bowie song "The Man Who Sold the World," because David Bowie is one of my favorite gender-fluid icons.

MARK: How are you dressing when you go to school?

DESMOND: I still wear what you'd call regular clothes to school, which used to be a plain T-shirt and pants, but now I am going to high school I want to be more out there with my fashion. But it will still be restrained. I don't wear makeup at school.

MARK: What pronouns do you use there?

DESMOND: My pronouns are "he," "she," or "them." At school it's generally "he." But I really don't care what you call me. I'm me.

MARK: Your makeup has got a lot more sophisticated over the last few years.

DESMOND: My mom and the internet taught me a lot and helped me evolve. I used to do really over the top makeup, and now I like something more casual. I like a smokey eye. Today I put black eyeshadow on, then smudged it, and used eyeliner and lip gloss. It's not drag every day now. There doesn't have to be a wig.

MARK: You've made a lot of appearances on television, and you did an interesting interview with the makeup artist Kabuki Starshine backstage after the February 2018 show by The Blonds. I remember taking Polaroids of Starshine at Jackie 60 in the 1990s when he was part of Susanne Bartsch's clique, and he then went on to do makeup on *Sex and the City*. He's so much a part of the fabric of New York downtown culture and fashion. What inspires you about him?

DESMOND: Kabuki was a real inspiration when I wanted to do over the top makeup. He's so creative, so talented. I first learned about him when I was finding out about the club kids of the late 1980s through to the 1990s. I loved their style, and how a lot of it was DIY. I encountered all that history by watching Nelson Sullivan's videos on YouTube. I'd searched to see what RuPaul looked like when he was first starting out and discovered Sullivan's stuff. Those videos are interesting because they show you what New York City and the queer community was like back in the 1980s. Kabuki did this really amazing makeup and I wanted to see if I could also do really unique makeup like his. Also, can I just say that Susanne Bartsch is amazing? I've met her a few times and she always looks really gorgeous.

MARK: Wendy, when do you remember when Desmond first became interested in fashion?

WENDY: I always watched classic Hollywood films, so he would watch them too—lots of films with costumes by Adrian. We also had a lot of magazines around the house. We used to buy him those little fashion sketch books and he'd draw in them, around six years old.

DESMOND: I remember us walking around SoHo and looking at Betsey Johnson's and Anna Sui's stores and finding everything about them so glamorous. Fashion is my favorite thing. Apart from trains. I love the whole history of trains. They were invented in 1804 in Wales. Ever since then, they have powered our world, and made cities grow. I want to move to London because the best railway stations in the world are there.

MARK: It's wonderful and eccentric that you want to move to London for that, and not for Charles Jeffrey or Simone Rocha. Which fashion designers do you like most?

Desmond is Amazing in Bushwick, New York.
Custom-made jumpsuit by BCALLA.

DESMOND: I will always love The Blonds, David and Phillipe Blond. Phillipe is like a supermodel and always wears amazing long blonde wigs. I wish I looked as beautiful as that. I was in the Disney Villains x The Blonds show at Fashion Week in September 2018 where Paris Hilton played Cruella de Vil, Dominique Jackson from *Pose* was Maleficent, and I was Diaval. That was one of the most amazing moments of my life.

I also like Miu Miu. I get off the bus right outside the Miu Miu store almost every day and I love the clothes—they're so cute. Also Anna Sui, Betsey Johnson, Alexander McQueen, Comme Des Garçons, Malan Breton, and Marc Jacobs. I recently saw a movie called *Love is in the Legend* (2020) and in it Marc was talking about walking in the vogue balls and how freeing it was. I also like Patricia Field because she has supported a lot of designers, and I appreciate people that use diverse models in their shows. I used to like Chanel before Karl died, but now it's not as good. If I could do runway for anyone it would be Dior.

MARK: What's the feeling you get when you're modeling? Because of your age, it always comes across as so playful and joyful.

DESMOND: I feel fabulous and amazing on the runway. It's one of my absolute favorite things. I've done a lot of modeling for magazine editorial too. I've been in *Vogue* four times, but for doing drag rather than modeling. It would be the biggest dream to model for them. I don't get nervous when I'm on a runway—it feels magical. It's a moment where I can show the world that someone like me can be a model.

MARK: Tell me about the book you put together about the history of Pride.

DESMOND: It took a long time to do. It was complicated but a success—I've seen a lot of kids on Instagram reading the book and that was my goal, to teach them about the LGBTQ community. I'm so proud of that. Next I want to write a book about the life of Barbette, an amazing trapeze artist who performed in drag, and then at the end of the show they would remove their wig and reveal that they were really a man.

MARK: How did you both, Wendy and Desmond, discover the history of the LGBTQ community?

WENDY: I had a favorite uncle growing up called Roger, who lived in California. He got AIDS and my mom and dad treated him like he had the plague. He would drink from a glass and my parents threw the glass away. Everyone was scared at the time, but I can't make excuses for them. It was traumatic. There was no gay marriage or equality back then, so when he died, his partner lost everything, he had no rights to the house. Roger has a square on the AIDS Memorial Quilt on block #4077. It has a quote from *La Cage Aux Folles:* "I am what I am. I am my own special creation." That has always stuck with me, and I think it is the best advice to live by. Even today when I think about what was lost during the AIDS epidemic I tear up. But it is comforting to know there is something left in the world of my uncle, and many others who lost their lives.

After Roger passed away, I vowed to be the best ally I could. Desmond was born prematurely on Pride weekend, at St. Vincent's Hospital in Greenwich Village, which was the hospital most associated with the AIDS epidemic. It felt like a sign. And here he is.

DESMOND: My mom got me to watch a lot of documentaries about Stonewall and how the government responded to the AIDS crisis.

WENDY: The country is still so divided today, and people on the right have a hangover from preconceptions about the LGBTQ community from the 1950s.

DESMOND: There are so many great people who should still be alive right now.

MARK: Wendy, when did you know Desmond wasn't just "going through a phase," as the cliché goes?

WENDY: It was when he was about age seven. He always played dress-up around the house—he would always watch *Drag Race* with me, and imitate by putting towels on his head for wigs and making accessories from stuff out of the recycling bin. All kids play dress-up—they make armor out of cardboard boxes—but Desmond always wanted to go into the little girl's department at department stores and showed me dresses that he wanted, and I knew it was more than just playing at dress-up.

When it came around to October that year, he wanted to go to the Village Halloween Parade as Elsa from *Frozen*. I needed to see how he felt on the street, and whether he was going to be okay. I'm still a protective mother. He strutted around at the parade and loved it. I was constantly asking myself around that time: "What if he is transgender? What would be harmful for me to do, or not to do?" Every parent faced with this also worries what people will think. You must learn to let go of that. Someone just doxxed us on Twitter again, giving out our home address, as an invitation to send hate mail. And I do care about that. But I've always wanted to give him the space to experiment. I don't want someone to be a mini-me. You need to make a child know they are valued.

I was raised Catholic, and I rebelled, and it was painful. It would have been better just to have been allowed to be an individual. When you rebel, you're not yourself, you're having to push harder than you would otherwise.

MARK: When you're a small boy and you have no idea about clothes being gendered, women's clothes always look more fun. Most boys play dress-up in their mother's or sister's clothes. Today I can wear one of my Rick Owens skirts, and because I'm middle-aged, six feet tall, and have gray hair and a beard, no one will dare say anything critical. But if you're a teenage boy with a slight build who dares wear anything seen as feminine, that invites aggression from people. I wonder if that's a reactionary impulse to try and thwart any sign of transgressive behavior when someone is still vulnerable and questioning themselves.

WENDY: It's about people being insecure. All boys dress up, but it's suppressed by their parents, and they aren't allowed to take that out of the house. It becomes a secret. Girls are allowed out as tomboys, but if boys are showing any traits of the "weaker sex," it's a problem.

MARK: I do think that's changing. Most of my friends with young children let their kids be as gender-fluid as they like. Being forced to conform is torturous, and it has been constantly reinforced to us through pop culture. If you go back to the mid-1980s, *The Breakfast Club* (1985) starts with the lyrics from David Bowie's "Changes" on screen—a song about teenage rebellion—but the film ends with Molly Ringwald's character, who wears a pink blouse, giving Ally Sheedy's character, who wears black, a makeover. She changes her identity to make her popular, and Sheedy's character subsumes her identity to achieve happiness. I also find it strange how wearing black was seen as suggesting introspection and sadness. Desmond, what's your take on black? Do you ever wear it?

DESMOND: I do. I wore a black outfit to Taco Bell last night. It's one of my favorite colors. But I always wear it with pink because it makes the pink really stand out.

Regine gown by Malan
Breton, 2019; flower
headpiece by Vivivalue.

Jacket by Theory, 2018;
shirt by Calvin Klein,
2021; ring, unsigned
(gifted by a fan).

Marlene gown by
Malan Breton, 2019.

Suit by OppoSuits, 2021;
tie bar by Alynn and tie
by Spring Notion.

Floral blouse,
unsigned, *c.* 1960s.

One of a kind
sequin sweater
dress by Richie
Rich, 2018; sheer
rhinestone shirt by
The Phluid
Project, 2018.

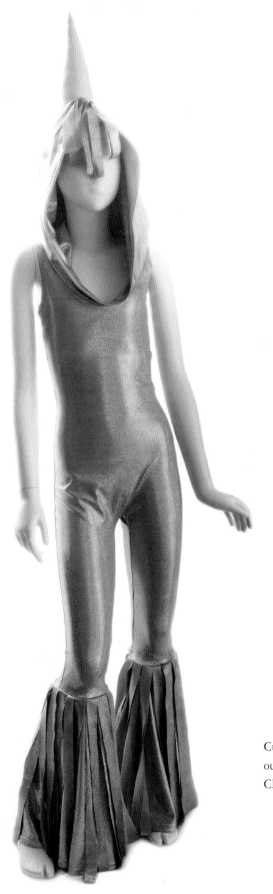

Custom-made unicorn
outfit by Coquetry
Clothing, 2021.

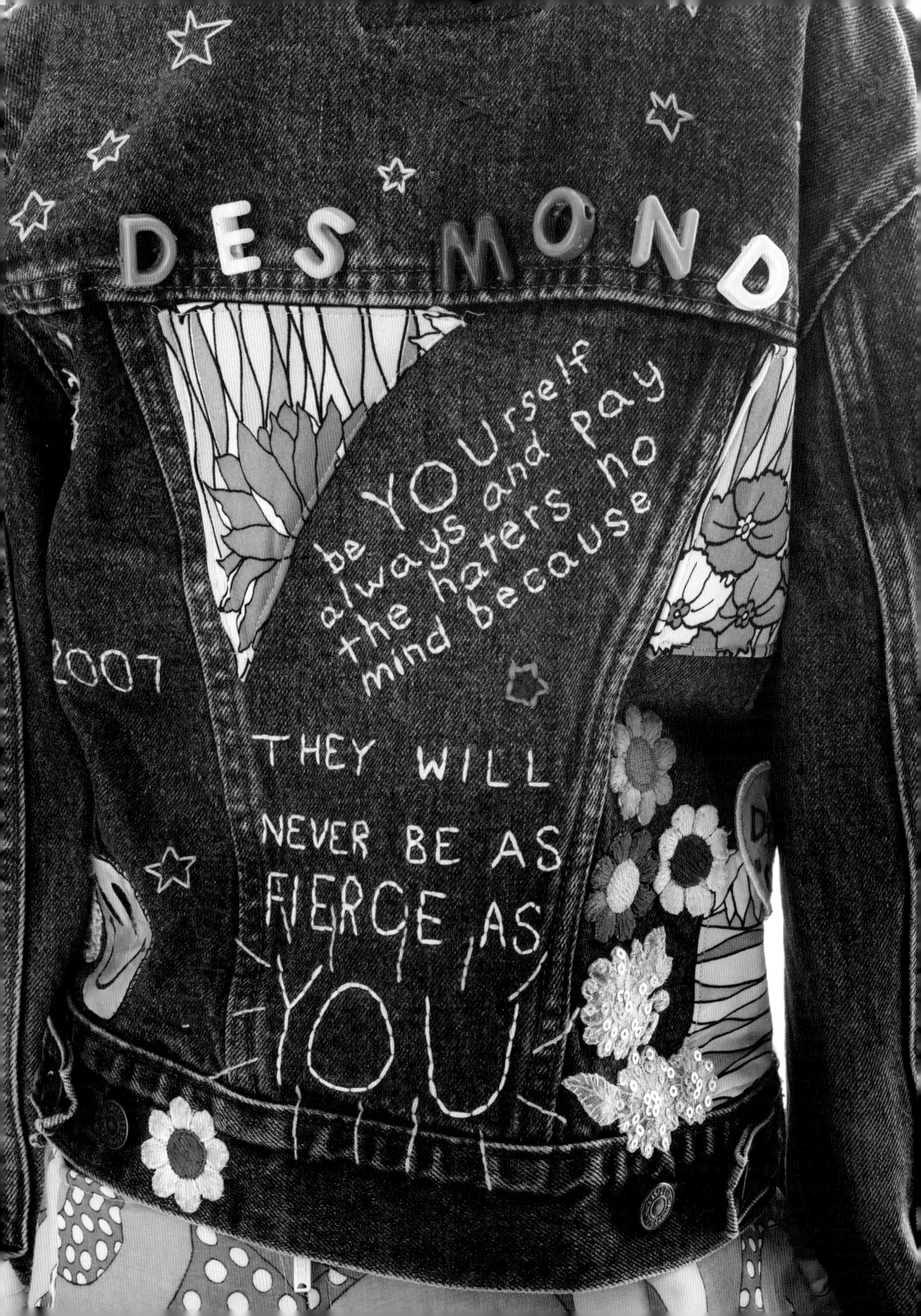
DESMOND
be YOUrself always and pay the haters no mind because
THEY WILL NEVER BE AS FIERCE AS YOU
2007

One of a kind hand-embroidered jacket by The Series, 2018; crop shirt made by Desmond; swimming shorts, unsigned, *c.* 1960s; Custom platform shoes by East Village Shoe Repair, using vintage Converse.

Sequined unitard by
Alexandra Collection,
2021; floral helmet
made by Desmond.

292

Index

Acknowledgments

With thanks to Neil D.A. Stewart for tireless support, advice, and editing, and Frances Arnold for endless encouragement and email counsel. Also: Guy Berryman, Silvia Bertocchi, Simon Costin, Michael Costiff, Paul Gorman, Andrew Groves, Norma Kamali, Michelle Kelly, Young Kim, Annika Lievesley, William Norwich, Rifat Ozbek, Jessica Pearson, Paige Powell, Becky Thomas, and Alistair and Vida Stewart for their support of the ever-growing John Skelton collection.

Mannequins for Winn Austin, Charlie Casely-Hayford, John Matheson and McQueen Vault, and Sandy Powell courtesy of Universal Display, with thanks to Jonathan Berlin in London.

Mannequins for Karim Rashid and Carla Sozzani courtesy of Bonaveri, with thanks to Erika Gabrielli in Renazzo, Ian Thompson at Blue Studio Trading London, and David Terveen at DK Display New York.

Special mannequin-related thanks also to N'ketiah Brakohiapa, David Halbout, and Anne Kong at FIT, New York.

Susanne Bartsch's makeup by Deney Adam; hair (full length) by Raquel Martuscelli; hair (portrait) by Charley Brown.

Carmen Haid's hair and makeup by Tania Gautama (London) and Marian Filali (Marrakech).

Sandy Powell's hair and makeup by Grayson Galway.

Heavy lifting in the studio, mannequin wrangling, styling, and crisis management: Elissa Collier-Cray, Timothy Gibbons, Yasemen Hussein, Brandon Olsen, Alice Pylypenko, and Nick Witchey.

Location angels: Kim Fraczek; Pete Goldring at Christ Church Spitalfields; Carmen Haid; Eleanore Longley at J/PR and all at The Beaumont in Mayfair; Maureen Mills and the management at Bob Bob Ricard in Soho; Eugene Rabkin; Antony Rettie at AKA Communications and all at Christopher's in Covent Garden; Zanna Dear and David Turner at the David Turner Workshop; and Chris Twaddle.

All photography by Mark C. O'Flaherty.